F.T Haig

Daybreak in North Africa

An Account of Work for Christ begun in Morokko, Algeria, Tunis, and

Tripoli

F.T Haig

Daybreak in North Africa
An Account of Work for Christ begun in Morokko, Algeria, Tunis, and Tripoli

ISBN/EAN: 9783744757256

Printed in Europe, USA, Canada, Australia, Japan

Cover: Foto ©Lupo / pixelio.de

More available books at **www.hansebooks.com**

DAYBREAK IN NORTH AFRICA.

An Account of

WORK FOR CHRIST BEGUN IN MOROCCO,

ALGERIA, TUNIS, AND TRIPOLI.

BY

MRS. F. T. HAIG.

LONDON:
S. W. PARTRIDGE & CO., 9, PATERNOSTER ROW, E.C.

DAYBREAK IN NORTH AFRICA.

North Africa Mission.

Council.

J. H. BRIDGFORD, Tunbridge Wells.
ALGERNON C. P. COOTE, Powis Square, W.
W. SOLTAU ECCLES, Upper Norwood, S.E.
EDWARD H. GLENNY, Barking.
GENERAL and MRS. F. T. HAIG, Redhill.
R. C. MORGAN, 12, Paternoster Buildings, E.C.
JAMES STEPHENS, Highgate Rise, N.W.
THEODORE WALKER, Leicester.

Office of the Mission.
19 AND 21, LINTON-ROAD, BARKING.

Hon. Treasurer.
W. SOLTAU ECCLES, Lyndhurst, Church Road, Upper Norwood, S.E.

Hon. Secretary.
EDWARD H. GLENNY, 21, Linton Road, Barking.

Assistant Secretary.
WILLIAM T. FLOAT.

Hon. Auditors.
ARTHUR J. HILL, VELLACOTT & CO., 1, Finsbury Circus.

Bankers.
LONDON AND COUNTY BANKING CO., 21, Lombard Street, E.C.

INTRODUCTION.

CHAPTER I.

Ho! every one that thirsteth, come to this fountain side!
Drink freely of its waters, drink and be satisfied!
Yet linger not, but hasten on, and bear to all around
Glad tidings of the love and peace and mercy thou hast found.

Then, as of old, in vision seen before the prophet's eyes,
Broader and deeper on its course the stream of life shall rise;
And everywhere, as on it flows, shall carry light and love,
Peace and goodwill to man on earth, glory to God above!

"THE FIELD IS THE WORLD." So said One whose every utterance was far-reaching and full of meaning. Born a Jew, and during His earthly life never passing beyond the narrow limits of the land of His birth, His spiritual vision took in all the kingdoms of the world, and His heart went out in yearning love and pity to the despised Gentile races unknown to, and uncared for by those around Him. His thoughts went forward to the time when His other sheep, not of that fold, should be gathered in; and they too were included in the intercessions of that last wonderful prayer in which the feelings of a lifetime were gathered up and poured out to His Father in heaven: "Neither pray I for these alone, but for them also which shall believe on Me through their word." His parting instructions to His disciples show plainly what His desires and intentions were with regard to all nations far and near, "Go ye into all the world, and preach the Gospel to every creature." And again, "Ye shall be witnesses unto Me unto the uttermost parts of the earth" (Acts i. 8).

This long-neglected and almost forgotten command is now being pressed upon the attention of Christians by many voices and many pens, and not in vain. Many are offering themselves to carry the sweet Gospel message wherever their Lord would have them go, and many others are waking up to perceive that the traditional guinea to this or that society is an absurdity which they no longer dare ask the Lord, who watches the gifts put into His treasury, to accept.

But is there not need for a further awakening? Have we yet learned to place ourselves by the side of our Blessed Master, and, looking out with Him over "The Field of the World," to see things from His point of view, although our eyes are so dim that they can at best take in but little of what He sees? Looking thus, should we not observe many things before unnoticed? Empty spaces where no labourer has gone would attract attention; other places, feebly attempted and ill supported, would arouse prayerful interest.

This thought is by way of apology to the reader for introducing a mission comparatively lately begun, little known, and as yet very poorly supported.

It is remarkable that when the thought of carrying the Gospel to other countries first suggested itself—rather, we should say, was borne in upon Christian hearts by the power of the Holy Spirit—to go to idolaters, and to the farthest parts of the earth seems to have been the first idea with all. India, the distant islands of the Pacific, South Africa, Madagascar, New Zealand, were among the first to attract labourers from our own country, while the Moravians had been before us in going to the Indians of America and the Greenlanders. The thought seems to have come only recently to those who are "lifting up their eyes and looking on the fields," that on the way to those far-off lands are others quite near and accessible, where the one only Saviour is unknown, and where Mahomedanism shuts out the light as effectually as the debasing idolatries of heathenism. It is, however, true that only at a comparatively late date, barriers have been removed which formerly made the northern shores of Africa inaccessible to Christian enterprise. It is difficult to realise that only sixty years ago Algiers was still a city of pirates, that indeed all the principal towns along the coast line of Algeria and Morocco were inhabited by fierce corsairs, whose business was to attack passing vessels, plundering, killing, or carrying away into a miserable slavery all who fell into their hands.

In A.D. 935 the city of Algiers was founded by an Arab prince, and from that time forward Islam seems to have been firmly established in the land. In A.D. 1492 the Moors, being driven from Spain, settled all along the north coast of Africa, and soon became known as a nation of pirates. Many expeditions were at different times fitted out against them, but all proved singularly unsuccessful. In 1541 the Emperor Charles V. landed in Algiers, with an immense fleet and army, but a fearful storm, with earthquakes and waterspouts, destroyed most of his ships and forced him to withdraw. Other later attempts to humble these proud pirates were invariably baffled.

Several European nations—Sweden, Denmark, Portugal, Spain, etc., were compelled to buy protection for their vessels by payment of an annual tribute. During the French Revolution there was a lull. The presence of large armed fleets in the Mediterranean hindered the pirates in their operations, but as soon as the war was over, they recommenced with fresh vigour. The first check given them was from the Americans, who attacked the Algerine fleet off Carthagena in the summer of 1815, defeated it, and compelled the Dey to respect the American flag. Soon after, Lord Exmouth demanded from all the States of Barbary, the recognition of international law which would insure some humanity towards prisoners. Algiers refused consent, and was bombarded by the united English and Dutch fleets, its naval force, and magazines being all destroyed. The Dey was at last forced to yield, being compelled to do so by his own soldiers, and a treaty was concluded, by which piracy and the slavery of Christians were renounced. The result was so far good, that 1,211 Christian slaves were delivered up to the British Admiral. But piracy was soon resorted to again, and was not fully put a stop to till the final Conquest of Algeria by the French in 1830.

The establishment of French rule in Algeria was the dawn of a new era for all Northern Africa; piracy has so completely died out along the whole of the coast line, that it seems now a forgotten state of things. In Algeria itself the conflict between the conquered and the conquerors raged long and fiercely. For nearly twenty years the attempt to shake off the yoke of their new masters was repeated continually; but since the complete crushing of the effort for independence led by Abdel Kader, and his banishment from the country, there has been no serious renewal of warfare. The people have quieted down, their conquerors have adopted a conciliatory policy, and their rule has been attended with many material benefits to the population. Roads and railways have been constructed, and in 1856 the French Government conferred a great boon upon the people by boring for water in several places.

A bountiful supply was procured by means of Artesian wells, which seemed to the simple people quite miraculous. They named the first well "Fountain of Peace," the next they called "Fountain of Blessing," and the third "Fountain of Gratitude." May these names be repeated in a deeper, fuller sense, as wells of Living Water spring up among them. "Spring up, O well, sing ye unto it" (Numbers xxi. 17); "I will open rivers in high places, and fountains in the midst of the valleys; I will make the wilderness a pool of water, and the dry land springs of water" (Is. xli. 18).

CHAPTER II.

ALGERIA.

Call them in, the poor, the wretched
Sin-stained wanderers from the fold:
Peace and pardon freely offer;
Can you weigh their worth with gold?
Call them in—the weak, the weary,
Laden with the doom of sin:
Bid them come and rest in Jesus;
He is waiting—call them in.

HUS, in the providence of God, the long-closed door of Northern Africa was opened, by which His servants might go in, carrying the everlasting Gospel. Not for long after that, however, did it come into any one's heart to do so. Algeria was soon resorted to by travellers for its picturesque beauty, and by seekers after health, because of its sunshine and its pleasant climate, but few, if any, gave a thought to the souls around them on whom the Light of Life had never shone. Perhaps some did feel for them, and send up in secret a cry for help to our Father who seeth in secret, which is now being answered.

Algeria has a history stretching far back into the past. Many races meet and mingle there now. The traveller arriving at Algiers has hardly time to admire the stately city, its white houses rising one above another on the slopes of an extensive semicircle of hills, before the steamer is surrounded by a flotilla of small boats, manned by a motley crew of Arabs, Kabyles, Spaniards, and Maltese, waiting to convey him from the vessel to the quay. Once landed,

"He is at first bewildered by the new persons, rather than by the new things about him. He feels suddenly transported into a masquerade, and can scarcely persuade himself that his surroundings are 'all real,' as Arab, Kabyle, Moor, and Jew passes by him, each in his curious Eastern dress."

In addition to the Eastern element, there is the European: the French colonists and officials, and a large number of Spanish settlers. Nor is the distinctively African type wanting, as there are many negroes and negresses, now released from slavery. There are also many Jews.

But of all these races the dwellers in the mountains in Eastern Algeria, called Kabyles, are perhaps the most ancient. They differ entirely from the Arab descendants of those Mahomedan invaders who poured into the country at different times when Islam was spreading itself in full strength and vigour. Professor Sayce speaks of the Kabyles as descendants of the ancient Libyans, and claims kindred for them with the Amorites of Canaan in a remote past, and with the fair Celts of an Irish village in the present. He says—

"The traveller who first meets with them in Algeria cannot fail to be struck by their likeness to a certain part of the population of the British Isles. Their clear, white, freckled skins, their blue eyes, their golden-red hair, and tall stature, are in striking resemblance to the modern Celt, and when we find that their skulls, which are of the 'long-headed' type, are the same as the skulls discovered in the prehistoric cromlechs of the country they still inhabit, we may conclude that they represent the descendants of the white-skinned Libyans of the Egyptian monuments."

Later traditions of this interesting people make it clear that at one time many, if not all their tribes, embraced the Christian faith, which they were forced again to renounce by their Mahomedan conquerors. The villages of the Kabyles are scattered over the mountains of Algeria, but it is the same race which, under the name of Riffs or Riflians, inhabit the wild country which is the borderland of Morocco, and, again, they are found in even greater numbers in the south and west of Morocco, where both the people and their language are called Shluh. All are included under the name of Berbers. Like other mountaineers, they are strong in their love of freedom, and long resisted the establishment of the French Government over them.

The attention of Christians was first attracted to this interesting race in 1876, when Mr. and Mrs. George Pearse visited Algiers in prosecution of their work among the French soldiers. During their stay there they had their first glimpse of the Kabyles from the windows of their hotel, which overlooked an open space where many of them used to congregate. The sight of these fine-looking mountaineers awakened the sympathies of hearts accustomed to seek the salvation of souls, and suggested the thought that something must be done to bring to them the light of life and salvation. An incident which occurred served to deepen this impression. There had been a

A KABYLE.

time of famine, followed by a terrible epidemic. Looking out from the window one bright moonlight night, Mrs. Pearse saw what at first she thought was a bundle of rags on a pavement under a wall, but which, on

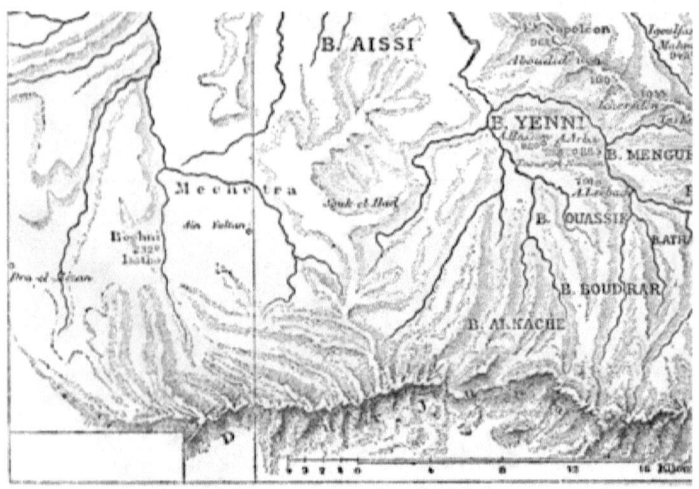

looking more narrowly, she saw was a man. Another lay near him, his ghastly face upturned to the moon. She could not go out to help them, it was two o'clock in the morning, and the house was locked up; she could only pray that help might come to them. In the morning at six, when the Arab water-carrier came, Mrs. Pearse asked him about those poor men. They were dead, unpitied, uncared for. Seeing her emotion, the man said, "Their fate affects me about as much as a dead dog would; I am used to it; hundreds have gone in a short time." The pitiful sight was graven upon Mrs. Pearse's mind, and the spiritual condition of these people presented itself very vividly to her—so neglected, so forgotten. It stirred her to earnest prayer, and she and her husband never rested till something was done to carry the Gospel to them.

French Protestants had at that time done nothing for the natives of Algeria, and Mr. and Mrs. Pearse naturally turned to English Christians. Coming to England, Mr. Pearse applied to the Church Missionary Society through the Rev. C. Fenn, to learn if it was possible for them to undertake a mission to the Kabyles, but that great Society felt it impossible to take up work so entirely new and distant from their existing missions.

Mr. Pearse, therefore, sought to interest Christians in general by publishing a short account of the Kabyles and his first journeys among them, much of which will still be read with interest. Touching on the past history of those lands he thus wrote:—

"Northern Africa has played an important part in the past, and was, in fact, the granary of the Roman Empire; and for three centuries, from Tertullian to Augustine, the Church of Christ there exercised a great influence in Europe and in the East. It suddenly emerged from obscurity in A.D. 198, when the apology for the Christian Faith was addressed by Tertullian to the Roman governors. The Church went on increasing in numbers till it had 579 sees, some of them, doubtless, being very small. It had, like other parts of the Roman Empire, its persecutions. In A.D. 258, Cyprian, Bishop of Carthage, was martyred, and in the same persecution the young African lady, Perpetua, was slain in the Colosseum, the remains of which now exist at Carthage. The Kabyles have been successively subject to the Carthaginians, Romans, Vandals, Turks, and now the French are their masters. The Romans could not master the rocks of Jur-jura, but they controlled the Kabyles by having military stations commanded by præpositi along the banks of the rivers Sahell and Sebaou. The Turks followed the same plan, and held possession of the country through their forts on these same rivers. Amongst their troops they had some negro auxiliaries, who were rewarded by having lands allotted to them. They settled down in separate villages, and were subsequently received into the Kabyle Confederation, and now live harmoniously amongst them. During the Roman dominion the people in the towns spoke Latin, but the country people the Punic tongue, traces of which are found in the Kabyle of the present day. There is no doubt that some Kabyle families are of Roman origin; for instance, the Abbekkar, a fraction of the village Iril G'Ifri, and others.

"It was during the second Saracenic invasion under Akba-en-Nefa, with his 10,000 horsemen, in the seventh century, that the Kabyles were made to submit to the Mussulman yoke and religion, and driven to their mountains; but it was about the time that the Turks arose in the thirteenth century that a desert tribe, the Beni Zian from Arabia, swept over North Africa, obtained possession of Central Moghreb, and again drove the aborigines into the mountains, or into the Sahara; and from this time dates the complete subjection of the people to the religion of their conquerors. Still, in some places their faith in Islam is very slight, and their knowledge of what the Koran really teaches still less."

After paying a visit to Algeria in 1879, Mr. H. Grattan Guinness was so deeply impressed with the spiritual destitution of the Kabyles, as totally unevangelised, that he urged upon Mr. and Mrs. Pearse the importance of undertaking a mission to them, and they soon after set out on a journey of exploration among the Kabyle villages. They went first to Constantine, and from thence to Setif, which is the centre of immense elevated plains, where wheat and other grains are largely grown, their object being to attend the weekly market at the latter places, where from 8,000 to 10,000 Arabs and Kabyles congregate from all the country round. Describing the scene, Mrs. Pearse wrote:—

"In they pour, on horses, mules, donkeys, and camels. What an imposing sight! The sunrise on the distant mountains imparting its glorious hues; the patient beasts of the desert with their stately tread, laden with corn, their young following them; Arabs on foot with their flocks. Here, in a vast square, goats, sheep, and oxen are disposed of. We rose at sunrise, and went out well stored with Arabic tracts and books, watching them gathering from every quarter. We looked about and prayed, feeling our nothingness and impotence amongst such a mass of untutored, wild, and illiterate men; but their bearing is dignified, and they are mostly fine men, and Mrs. Grimké's Arabic illustrated cards made them smile and show their white teeth. But how sad they look! Although their Koran recognises the Seidna Aïssa as the Eternal Word, born of the Virgin, yet they do not know Him as a Saviour.

"The mounted Arab police, in their red cloaks, kept order. On one side

SÉTIF.

there was a circle formed around an Arab reciting a long poem, the inner circle seated on the ground in deep abstraction, and the outer standing around them. The improvisatore, with an animated countenance and fiery eye, went on with great rapidity, and every one apparently was fascinated by the recitation.

"We thought it best to begin our distribution with the shepherds, who, though they may not all read, can generally find some one who will. At first they seemed rather suspicious of us, but when they found we were 'Inglese' they accosted us in an unintelligible language. Soon our tempting little books (pink, blue, and green) were produced, and, like sheep, they followed one after another, and began to be eager to get them, and we heard 'Donnez' on all sides, the gamins being very pertinacious, full of fun and frolic, as everywhere. We noticed several fine, intelligent young men, who could read well, and they asked us to give explanations about the books, of which we gave them the best we had. One kissed the leaves with the sacred characters.

"Then we got amongst the goats, and the owners had to beat off the crowd which pressed around. Now we went amongst the horned cattle and mules. Not a heel moved, nor a horn pushed us, and we felt that we could have kept amongst them for hours, and that the Lord was with us. Great was our joy in being able to look our swarthy brethren in the face, a long-felt desire now granted, and it was very evident no such thing had ever been done amongst them. Now we can understand, in the presence of such masses of Christless souls, how our Lord had compassion on the multitudes who were as sheep without a shepherd."

Leaving Setif, Mr. and Mrs. Pearse travelled on through a part of Eastern Kabylia, through a grand country, where in places the road was cut out of the sides of immense mountains, 5,000 and 6,000 feet high. Again Mrs. Pearse wrote:—

"How my heart has bled in contemplating the position of the Kabyle women! Whenever we came to a village the women hid themselves; the young girls, some remarkably beautiful, fled like wild gazelles. A large part of the work in the fields falls on the women. Passing along the side of a mountain, we heard a murmur of voices from the valley below. It came from a number of women and girls, employed in the various processes of making oil, drying the olives, crushing, pressing, and washing at a spring issuing from a rock. I saw one struggling along under a load of wood. A wife is purchased at about the same price that would be given for a good mule, say 500 fr. Though a Kabyle has only one wife, she is no companion for her husband. His place of resort is the Djemaa, a kind of public club-room at the entrance of the village, fitted with stone seats all round it, where the men meet to rest and to discuss the affairs of the village world. One reads the thrilling narratives by Christian sisters in China and India of their work amongst the women and girls. The poor neglected women amongst the Kabyles need the sympathy and help of English women, and it does not require a long voyage to reach them."

The Lord was drawing out the hearts of His servants to care for those who were sitting in darkness and the shadow of death, and at first the most hopeful and attractive field of labour appeared to be amongst this ancient people, in the villages scattered over the mountains of Algeria, so that the effort for their benefit, soon to be begun, was at first called " A Mission to the Kabyles and other Berber races." Subsequent experience has shown that it is impossible to separate one of the mixed races of North Africa from another in carrying the Gospel to them, and the Kabyles have not proved as accessible as some others. The present title of "North Africa Mission" is therefore more exactly suitable to the work as it has developed.

After several journeys and sojourns among the Kabyle villages, to gain information and to test the kind of reception likely to be accorded to mission-workers sent among them, a beginning was made in 1881 by a young Swiss (M. Mayor) and a converted Druse (Selim Zaytoun) settling at Djemaa Sahridj, and at the same time Mr. Edward Glenny was led to undertake the supervision and development of the work while residing in England.

Mr. Pearse had greatly wished that an industrial, self-supporting mission might be formed, and it was with this in view that Mr. Glenny was first led to go to Algeria and make careful inquiries as to the possibilities of such a scheme. He was led to decide against it, and seeing how God has permitted the Mission, within these few years since its commencement, to spread west and east, first into Morocco, and next into Tunis and Tripoli, we cannot but see His guiding hand which thus prevented it from being localized, and probably cramped in its operations.

About the same time the Bible Society's agent, Mr. Lowitz, opened a depôt for the sale of Scriptures in the town of Algiers, and shortly after, Mr. Mackintosh, a missionary who had laboured in Syria until failure of health compelled him to retire, but whose heart was still in the work, and who had become interested in Morocco by meeting some of the natives of that country on pilgrimage to Mecca, offered his services to the Bible Society for Morocco. He was sent there at first to pioneer, but afterwards as a permanent agent.

OLIVE GATHERING.

He also had thus been led providentially, but quite independently, to care for the needs of North Africa.

It is needless now to dwell upon the hopes and disappointments connected with the first beginnings of the Mission. The latter were not wanting; but looking back over the eight years that have passed since the commencement of the effort, we can but say, "What hath God wrought!" At the present time there are fifty-one missionaries occupying twelve different stations in connection with the North Africa Mission, besides a number of independent workers, several of whom began work with the help of the Society, but afterwards preferred working on separate lines. Manifest tokens of God's blessing have here and there been given, and souls have been gathered into the heavenly garner, there to join the great company of the redeemed, washed in the blood of the Lamb, who but for this Mission would never have heard of the Saviour of sinners. It is true there are immense difficulties to be encountered.

"The North Africa Mission," writes Mr. Glenny, "had no child's play before it when it endeavoured to carry the Gospel to Mohammedans, and to that part of the world where Mohammedanism had most completely triumphed over Christianity, and had for more than a thousand years held undisputed sway over Berbers and Arabs alike. The false teachings of Islam had, in more than thirty generations, permeated the social and political, as well as the religious life of the people, and thus they had become much more difficult to reach than the untutored savage, or even the dupes of Rome. Had not God in His mercy already to a great extent dried up the political power of Mohammedanism, it would have been impossible to re-evangelise North Africa. The fact that it is possible has come as a revelation to almost every one. Even yet the Church is not awake to the fact, and is acting as though Moslem political power was the same now as half a century ago, and the evangelisation of its victims still impossible. Everywhere almost, Mohammedan power is passing, and must pass away."

It *must*, for the mouth of the Lord hath spoken it, and even now places which used to be closed, as it were, with gates of brass and bars of iron to any breath of Christian truth, are thrown open, that the feet of them that bring good tidings, and that publish peace, may enter in. Yet still sufferings, and even death, await the convert who believes in his heart, and desires to confess with his mouth the Lord Jesus. The cruel beatings which some converts have had to endure, and the shrinking back of others even after baptism because unable to face the persecution which they saw lay before them, show plainly the need, the pressing need there is that we at home should help by faith and prayer our brethren and sisters who are carrying on the warfare. When Moses' hand was let down, Amalek prevailed, and only while it was held up Israel prevailed. Do we realise how much depends on us? how the conflict with the powers of evil which is going on down in the valley has its victories or threatened defeats influenced by our faithfulness or slackness in prayer, as we look on from the quiet mountain side, out of reach of the toil and the danger of the battle? A missionary in Korea lately wrote: "Just now the obstacles do seem somewhat formidable; I want you to pray the obstacles down, or pray us above them." Faith, which includes prayer, subdues kingdoms and removes mountains.

CHAPTER III.

MISSION STATIONS IN ALGERIA.

Dying? Yes, dying in thousands,
  A hopeless, despairing death;
Can we not hear them calling,
  Pleading with bated breath:
" Will no one come over and bring us light?
Must we perish in darkness darker than night?"

Dying! In loveless silence;
  For there is none to tell
The only message that comforts—
  The message we know so well—
That the God of love who gave His Son,
Hath given Him freely for every one.

Dying! while we are dreaming
  In selfish idleness;
Unconscious that those darkened lives
  Are so full of bitterness.
Oh, brothers and sisters for whom Christ died,
Let us spread His message far and wide.

DJEMAA SAHRIDJ.

THE first Mission station was opened at Djemaa Sahridj, which occupies a charming situation at the foot of the first spurs of the Jur-jura, and has been called the Damascus of Kabylia, the "country of springs," as its name signifies. It has consequently a perennial freshness amongst its many gardens. It has a mosque of Saracenic construction, and in the market-place is a well-built stone basin, receiving the waters of a magnificent spring. A large market is held on Fridays, and the people are of a busy and active disposition. The village, consisting of 3,000 persons, is made up of rather heterogeneous elements, and there are a considerable number of Marabout families—the Marabouts being hereditary Mahomedan teachers. Here, on a prominent hill, 1,165 feet above the river Sebaou, stands now a little whitewashed Mission-house. It is just outside the village, and overlooks a wide extent of country, the windings of the river Sebaou, and a range of mountains stretching to the left and right. Here during the year 1882, or a part of it, resided Mons. Mayor, with his Syrian helper, Selim Zaytoun. But the difficulties which met them at the outset were great. The French authorities, suspecting some political aim, forbade their teaching a number of Kabyle young men who had gathered around them; and also forbade their helping the sick with medicines as they were not "diplomés." Under the pressure of trials and difficulties, Zaytoun left the country, and M. Mayor also left for a time, but has since returned, and is now working independently in a Kabyle village. The work, however, was not abandoned. In October, 1883, Mr. and Mrs. Lamb, with their three little children, landed in Algiers, and at once proceeded to Djemna Sahridj, where they laboured until 1889, when they moved on to another station.

Before the arrival of Mr. Lamb and his family, two ladies, Miss Gillard and a friend, had gone there for a time, and afterwards moved to a village higher up the mountains. There they have built a small cottage of two rooms, having first of all tried living in a Kabyle house, but that they found too contrary to all ideas of health or comfort. Miss Gillard has lived there now for seven years, working quietly and persistently, teaching the children, nursing the sick, and thus trying to win a way for the words of eternal life.

After a time Mr. Lamb was joined by M. Cuendet, a Swiss, who, a year later, brought a young Swiss bride to add to the Mission party. Later on, Mr. and Mrs. Lamb went to open a new Mission station at Akbou, while the older station was reinforced by two ladies, Miss Smith and Miss Cox.

In every country where a new and difficult language has to be acquired, the early years of a Mission must needs be a time of patient preparation; even sowing the seed of the Word cannot be done to any extent until the language has been mastered, and in the case of an un-written language like the Kabyle, there are special difficulties in the way of acquiring it. The great want of the Scriptures translated ready to hand also makes itself felt. It is both a hindrance and a help that French is so much spoken in all the more accessible parts of Algeria, Kabyle villages included, that a good conversational knowledge of French has been found a primary necessity to all missionaries going there, thus making an additional tax upon their time. It has this advantage, that by means of French, they can speedily get into communication with a portion of the inhabitants; but this hardly makes up for having to acquire two foreign languages at once. A Gospel of John in the Kabyle language, and printed in Roman characters, they found ready to hand, it having been translated by a German, Dr. Sauerwein. M. Cuendet has spent much labour on a translation of the Gospel of Luke. He and Mr. Lamb have also prepared translations of several passages of Scripture, which they are able to read to those with whom they come in contact; also about twenty hymns, the singing of which is always an attraction. Without having studied medicine, Mr. Lamb finds himself often able to relieve suffering by means of simple remedies, and the help thus given obtains for him many an invitation and hearty welcome into Kabyle houses. The following are a few of his experiences :—

"I have been to the village of Aigoussi Bonafir. In a public place, commanding a charming view, I sat, surrounded by a company of men, chief among whom was the Sheikh and leading Marabout of the mosque. As soon as I made known that I had medicine, one after another came seeking relief, some bringing their little children. Several gladly accepted Gospels in Arabic, among them the Sheikh, who seemed much pleased with it, and sat for some time reading it, and assenting to what I said regarding Christ as the Saviour of the world and Son of God. After more than an hour spent here, I was invited to visit several persons in their homes. One of them kindly prepared cous-cous* for me, and we ate together.

"On Sunday afternoon I visited the village of Meslouh, about three-quarters of an hour's distance from Djemaa Sahridj. When there, several women and children came round me, to whom I gave medicine. I endeavoured to make known the Gospel, both by reading portions of Scripture in Kabyle and speaking of God's love. Between Djemaa and Meslouh there are some detached Kabyle houses. From one of these an old man came, asking me to go and see a sick child. While on my way there I met a woman with a pitcher of water on her head, who said the child was hers, and, accordingly, led me to her house. I was quite taken with the little baby boy of five months, and was struck with the pleasure the old man had in the child as it

* Cous-cous is the national dish both of Algeria and Morocco; it is made of wheat flour, granulated in some way, and afterwards steamed along with meat and vegetables.

turned its little face to him, and he, calling it by name, kissed it. These poor but grateful people gave me a few large pomegranates. The old man, and several who had gathered about the door, listened intently as I spoke of the Lord Jesus. An expression, employed by the Kabyles in wishing one another recovery from some bodily ailment, I have adopted, with an addition which generally calls forth surprise. They say, 'Adirk Rebbi Thabbourth,' *i.e.*, 'God give you the door (healing),' to which I add, 'R'efoud 'em Sidna Aissa,' which means, 'in the face of the Lord Jesus,' or for Jesus' sake. Their expression, 'in the face of,' recalls Psalm lxxxix. 9, 'Look upon the face of Thine anointed.'"

The work at this station is still carried on very quietly, in spite of many hindrances. A class for Kabyle boys, who are learning in the French school, was attempted, in order to teach them from the Scriptures, on Sundays and Thursdays, and their bright intelligent faces were cheering to the teachers' hearts; but just as they began to learn a little, it was forbidden by the French authorities. A few little Kabyle girls were gathered to learn to sew and sing hymns; that also was put a stop to. And so was a meeting for men, held by M. Cuendet in the Djemaa, or place of public resort. M. Cuendet still visits the villages round, and has opportunities there and in Djemaa Sahridj itself of speaking and reading to individuals and small groups, and thus the knowledge of God's great salvation through Jesus Christ is being spread, slowly but surely.

Miss Smith and Miss Cox having been two and a half years in the work, are now able to converse pretty easily in Kabyle, and they are heartily welcomed by the women in their own houses.

"Everywhere the dear women and children welcome us, and there amongst these hidden ones, we find ample work. Indeed there is far more work in Djemaa Sahridj than we can ever do. The village contains nearly 3,000 inhabitants, besides which we are surrounded by other Kabyle villages, easy of access, where we are always welcomed. The girls of the lower class are from their earliest years despised and outcast, with the hardest work, and no instruction whatever. These poor children live a loveless life indeed, until sometimes at the early age of ten (often younger), the father or brother of the poor little one decides to sell her to a strange man, old enough often to be her father or grandfather. After this the girl is little better than a slave in the house of her husband. When he rides, she walks, while he is resting she is doing the most menial work of all kinds. Not only this, but if she fails to please her lord, she can be sold again, and even separated from her children. The Kabyle woman of the higher class is gentle and timid, and very sweet-looking, but her fate is hardly less hard than that of her poorer sisters. Certainly her work is less hard—making cous-cous and burnouses being considered Kabyle accomplishments; but then she is a prisoner for life. If her husband possesses no garden in connection with his house, this poor

A KABYLE GIRL.

young creature is enclosed within its dreary four walls, or if by any chance she does go out, it is mounted on a mule, her face entirely covered with a black veil.

"In one quarter a most interesting work seems commencing; a number of these dear women and children really desiring to learn the hymns, singing with us, and repeating the Bible words after us.

"On Sunday we visit the surrounding villages, M. Cuendet preaching, we assisting with the hymns.

"Madame Cuendet is always ready to give us a helping hand, but naturally her work is chiefly with her three little children, the eldest being not much more than three years old. We have been forced for some time to give up our work in the houses of the people, as small-pox has been and still is raging in the village. In nearly all Kabyle houses there is but one room. There on the floor lie the sick and dying, all huddled together; they take simply no precautions, all washing their clothes at the same fountain, and carrying the children about all covered with this terrible disease.

"We have recommenced our work in the French village of Mekla, have a class for children first and then for adults; but the opposition is great. If we depended in the very least on any efforts of our own, we should say the work is impossible; but happily it is all His work, we are but instruments. Oh, that friends at home would pray even more earnestly that we may be instruments He can abundantly bless, sanctified and meet for the Master's use!"

Let us also pray that God will grant to our friends "favour and good understanding" with the French authorities. In Paris the benefit resulting from Mr. McAll's efforts to bring the Gospel to the French "ouvriers" is so fully recognised that he was a few years ago presented with a medal by the "Société Nationale d'Encouragement au Bien," and again by a National Education Society, in token of their appreciation of the good done; and police authorities have cordially testified to the increased order and quiet in the neighbourhood of the Salles de Conference. In Algeria also the officials need only to be convinced that our missionaries truly desire to do good, and have no political aims, and we believe that they would give to their work the same encouragement that is accorded to it in other parts of France. For every hindrance that arises we have the resource of prayer, and we know that as the mountains flow down at the presence of our God, so will mountains of difficulty melt away when He clears the way for us. May He increase our faith, and awaken all His children to a sense of their responsibility as helpers to the brethren and sisters who are in the midst of the battle.

Tlemcen.

Two years after a commencement had been made in Djemaa Sahridj, a young Frenchman, M. Bureau, who had been converted in one of Mr. McAll's

Salles de Conférence in Paris, was sent to Tlemcen with the view of making that a permanent station if it should be found practicable. Tlemcen is 400 miles distant from Djemaa Sahridj on the western side of Algeria, and is strongly occupied by a French garrison, being their frontier position towards Morocco. The mountains which divide the two countries, and which are inhabited by Riffs, another branch of the Berber race, are only about ten miles distant, the town itself being built on the side of a mountain about two thousand six hundred feet above the sea. Being so high, the climate is very cold in winter, though hot in summer—as cold as England during December, January, and February, but without its comforts, while during spring and summer a blast of sirocco from the Sahara often brings excessive heat. The town is picturesque, surrounded by groves of olives, and with many outlying villages. The townspeople are chiefly Arabs, though some of them are of Berber origin, with a few Turks. The Arabs of Tlemcen are of a very superior and refined type, which character, with the touch of French civilisation that the men have received, makes them very friendly towards the missionaries. The French element in the population is considerable, and there are enough of Protestants for them to have a church with a resident pastor, an advantage not often enjoyed by them in Algeria. M. Bureau was removed when he had acquired a fair knowledge of Arabic to begin work in Tunis, and Tlemcen was successively occupied by several new missionaries, so that only very recently has actual work been begun in it. Mr. and Mrs. Marshall are now stationed there, with three ladies. Miss Read and Miss Day, who have been there longest, have access to more houses than they can find time to visit. They began by giving medical help to a few, which greatly opened the hearts of the Arabs to them. After about six months this was prohibited by the authorities on the ground of Miss Read not having a French diploma, but the entrance gained was never lost again, those with whom they have made friends introducing them to others.

"At present," says Miss Read, "we could visit two hundred houses if we only had the time. I will not say that in all these our teaching is acceptable. While they think we read and sing the Gospel to them for our own pleasure, all is well, but when we apply it to *them* many close the ear. Then there are some who would be willing to listen, but their husbands, knowing we want to convert them, forbid our reading in their houses, at the same time welcoming us. Altogether, visiting the women in their homes is hopeful, especially as they are so secluded. About two years ago we started a Sunday morning meeting for the poorer class of Arab men and women, Miss Day and I taking them in separate rooms. Six months after, finding this succeed, we invited these people to come on Friday afternoons also to a Gospel meeting. We get on an average from twenty to twenty-five men and women. They listen with perfect attention to the address, join in the hymns, which by frequent attendance they learn by heart, but though we kneel in prayer they remain seated. Among the children we are able to do something. We have had for two years a boys' Bible-class on Thursday afternoon. The boys are from four to thirteen years old, and the average attendance is twenty-four, though there are many more names on the books. The hour they spend with us we give to singing hymns, learning a text, and we tell them a short Bible story. We know that they repeat in their homes what they learn. On Tuesday afternoon we have a needlework class, teaching girls to make their own native garments. One hour we spend at needlework; then, work put away, we have half-an-hour singing Gospel hymns. This class has increased to our utmost limits, notwithstanding the teaching of hymns. For the sake of the needlework the parents like the children to come, and at present we have as many as we can possibly teach, and we take no new comers. The girls learn our hymns, and we cannot tell where their influence will end. 'Cast thy bread upon the waters, and thou shalt find it after many days,' is a precious promise to us, and the word of our God is ever sure. We have not accomplished anything of ourselves, it is the Lord's working. We do praise Him specially for persevering grace—grace to persevere in the work, and to persevere in prayer for it. Often we have been very downcast at the failure of our efforts to get the people to come to us. Some suspected us of evil motives in gathering the children to our house, others knew the true motive, and that was the stumblingblock, but now we have by the Lord's help a steady work in their midst, and having sown the seed, we look to the Lord to give the increase. The soil *is* hard, but praise the Lord that it is not harder."

The following account of an Arab family in Tlemcen is by Miss Vining, who spent some time there before taking up work in Oran :—

"Visited in the afternoon. While with Zorah she told me that her husband had been ill three days, and they had no money; but she said, 'Yesterday I prayed to Sidna Aisa, and said, "My husband is ill and cannot work, send us some money, or some food to eat,"' and she added, 'soon after my husband got up and said he would go and see if he could find a job, and in half an hour he brought fourpence. I was so glad, and so was he.' She gave me a large pomegranate, saying he had bought four for a sou (halfpenny), and after giving one to her, and one to Fatima, and putting one aside for himself, he gave her the fourth and best to give to me when I came. Their simple love and generosity in their deep poverty are very touching, and very precious to me, it is so true.

32 *ALGERIA.*

"Visited Zorah in the afternoon, and had a nice long talk with her. She is growing in grace, and beginning not only to pray, but to look for the answers. I said something about the sinfulness around us in the world, and she replied, 'Yes, there is sin, much sin, but Jesus can cleanse it away. I

INTERIOR OF KABYLE HOUSE.

pray to Him always, morning and evening, and I know He hears.' What joy such words must give to Him!

"Poor blind Fatima has wounded one of her feet lately, treading on a piece of glass in the street, and I promised her a pair of shoes with the next money 'Sidna Aisa' sent me. When I went to take the money the child was sitting on the steps, so I passed into the room, and after talking a little with her mother, I said, 'Fatima, the money has come for your shoes.' She sprang up, and with a perfectly radiant face threw both arms round my neck and kissed me. This is the greatest expression of joy and gratitude. Both she and her mother said, 'Jesus is good. He sent the money.' Now Zorah says she cannot keep Fatima in the house, she is always wanting to go out to wear her shoes. It is a simple thing, but as much joy and pleasure to this poor blind Arab girl of twelve years as a watch and chain would be to one of her age in England."

One more little incident of the work among the children, given by Miss Read, must be told before passing on : —

"We are having colder weather just now, and were hoping the small-pox would have abated, but it is as bad as ever, and we find it so difficult to assure the people that we sympathise with them, because we feel it right to refuse to go in when we know that the disease is in the house. One little girl of three years old, who had been coming with her parents to the meeting ever since she could speak, fell ill with this terrible scourge. One day her mother came to say she was crying for me, would I just go and look at her. I was not afraid for myself, but for others; but making up my mind to have a long walk afterwards, I went. Directly I entered the room she lifted her head from the mat where she was lying and said, 'She's come, she's come!' and then to me, 'Take me in your arms and sing "Jesus loves me."' I could not resist the little one's pleading, so took her up in the coverlet and sang to her, and she nestled in my arms and went to sleep—the first time for a week, her mother said. The next day I had a cold and headache, and other symptoms of small-pox; but, praise the Lord, these passed away, and we are all keeping well."

There are babes among the little Arab children whom the Lord Jesus would love to take in His arms and lay His hands on them and bless them, but, dear Christian women of England, they need you to bring them to Him.

CONSTANTINE.

The City of Constantine is the capital of the province of the same name. It is connected by railway with the port of Philippeville, which is about fifty miles distant. It has been for many centuries an important fortress, and one of the natural strongholds of a country frequently disturbed by wars and revolutions. Its ancient name was Cirta, the city of the Massisylan kings two or three hundred years before Christ. Narva, whose wife was a sister of Hannibal, was king B.C. 230. It is celebrated also in ecclesiastical history as a place to which Cyprian was banished A.D. 257. In A.D. 412 Sylvian, Primate of Africa, held a Council here, at which the celebrated Augustine assisted.

The situation of the city is very remarkable; it occupies the summit of a plateau of rock, whose surface slopes towards the south. On the north-west side the rocks rise perpendicularly nearly a thousand feet from the bed of the river Roummel. It is separated on the east from the surrounding country by a deep ravine, across which the French have thrown a handsome bridge, which now affords the only way of access to the city.

The population is between 30,000 and 40,000, and as it is the residence of the General, Prefect, and other high functionaries, it has a considerable French as well as native population. There is a French pastor here to care for the French Protestants, and the British and Foreign Bible Society have a colporteur in the province, who makes this his headquarters. In 1886, Mr. Pos, a Dutch gentleman, with his wife, was sent by the N.A. Society to take up work in the City of Constantine, but their health failing them, they were obliged to leave, and it has since been occupied by two ladies, Miss Colville and Miss Granger. Their work is carried on in much the same way as that of the sisters in Tlemcen—visiting the women in their homes and receiving all who will come to their house. Not long after they were able to converse a little in Arabic they were visited frequently by a Moslem, who became deeply interested in the Scriptures. For some months he regularly attended their meetings for reading and prayer, and seemed to drink in the truth, his growth in grace being evident to those who watched and prayed over him. Early in 1888 Miss Colville proposed to him to go to Tunis, that the brethren there might have an opportunity of judging as to the reality of his profession. This he did, delighting them all by his simple faith, his intelligent grasp of the Scriptures, and his earnest spirit, the result being that ere he left Tunis he was baptised by M. Bureau. This man was a native of Tagaste, the birthplace of Augustine.

The following extracts are from Miss Colville's journals:—

"Went to take dinner with a French lady and her Arab husband; they were both exceedingly kind. He is such a nice Arab; his native town is Fez, which he left when he was quite young. We had a nice talk with them both, and were surprised to find that she is even more ignorant than her husband of spiritual things. They were so interested when we spoke to them, and seemed anxious to hear. Called on another French lady, whose husband is an Arab.

"In the afternoon, when a little cool, visited the house we were in last week. There are four families; one of the men is a Haj, also his wife—that is, they have made the pilgrimage to Mecca. We sat in one room, and three women and two girls came while we talked to them and read some hymns, which they liked; and on finishing 'Rock of Ages' one of the women took the book and ran down to the Haj with it. We afterwards went down to the courtyard, when the Haj came and asked us to sit with him and his wife, which we did. He and the man to whom we had given John's Gospel had been up one night reading it, and had now got to the eleventh chapter, so we thought we were going to have a discussion, as he held our hymn-book in his hand; instead of which he seemed very interested, and said the hymns were good, but that Jesus did not die, as another had taken his place. I told him it was necessary *one* should die for all, and Jesus had completed our salvation on the Cross, and asked him to accept a Gospel, which he gladly did. He and the other man looked through it, and made remarks to each other, and several times asked us questions. They are two intelligent men, and we felt a little nervous to encounter them, but the Lord put the words in our mouths, and was our strength in weakness.

"The Arab woman we have to wash our floors told us a young girl was dead near us. We had heard the tum-tum going, and knew some one was dead. She said she would like to go and visit them, so we told her to go. She soon returned, telling us she had entered and told them she would like to bring us, so we went, and found the house full of women, as the family is rich. The body had just been carried out, dressed in silk brocaded with gold. She was seventeen years of age, and had died of consumption—a common disease here. She was to have been married very soon, and her grandmother had made all her clothes, and bought quantities of jewellery for her, as her father and mother are both dead. We looked into one room, and saw about forty women round the room, dancing and smiting their breasts and foreheads, tearing their cheeks, and shouting in a wild manner, 'O sidi! O sidi!' The tum-tum was in the centre of the room. The grandmother and three negroes and the little sister were sitting close to it repeating the same words. It was a heathenish sight; the perspiration and blood streamed down their faces and arms, and they had kept this up since daybreak yesterday—nearly two days. Our hearts went out in pity for these poor creatures, and wondered why we have been so highly favoured. What can we render to the Lord for all His benefits? We wish some in dear old England could be transported into these houses, and see these dear women, so precious to the Lord Jesus; I feel sure they would not desire to return, but would feel constrained to stay and dwell among them."

MASCARA AND MOSTAGANEM.

ARAB SHOEBLACK.

At Mascara Mr. and Mrs. Cheeseman were stationed for a time, but feeling the want of a more thorough knowledge of Arabic, Mr. Cheeseman went to reside in Oran, that he might study in the Government College there. He has now returned to Mascara, which is in the centre of a great plain, where many wandering tribes pitch their tents. Mr. Cheeseman has, after much difficulty, obtained a license as a colporteur, and his desire is to itinerate much among the villages and encampments, both selling the Scriptures and telling the Gospel message to all who will hear it.

At Mostaganem Mr. and Mrs. Liley have resided about two years. They have had many trials through ill-health and other discouragements, and need our prayers, as their post is a lonely one. Mr. Liley has a class of Arab shoeblack boys, and these are often a cheer to him. He writes:—

"I had the pleasure of meeting my class of shoeblacks, who now number thirty-two. I read to them the story of the Crucifixion, and explained why it was necessary that Christ should die for us. The interest they showed was quite encouraging.

"The first thing this morning an Arab came, to whom I had promised a Bible. His is a very hopeful case, and I believe the Lord is going to save his soul. Every evening he reads in a native café to a number of Arabs, who gather to listen. For nearly two hours I was in conversation with him about his soul, and he seemed very anxious to know the truth. The 'weeds and ivy vine' of old customs, however, cling tightly to him. As he left the house with the Bible, he said, 'I shall take this Bible home and read it carefully. As I read I shall ask God to show me the truth."

Later on, Mr. Liley took a short journey through the Dahra, a large district to the east of Mostaganem.

"Leaving Mostaganem early Friday morning, it was my intention to visit two large douars (encampments) near Pont de Cheliff, then continue my journey on foot to Bosquet. It was a disappointment to me to have to pass them in the diligence, which now meets the trains at Ain Tideles, and instead of passing these douars at 9 a.m. as formerly, it now passes them about midday. The heat was intense, 97° in the shade. It would have been folly for me to have visited the douars at this hour and in such heat. Arriving at Ain Ouillis, I visited the Protestants there; they are very poor, but sincere Christians. While in the house of one, an Arab entered, who was afterwards found to be the chief of a douar. As I spoke to him of Jesus Christ he looked at me in astonishment, repeating often, 'These words are good.' As he could read, a New Testament was given him. He would have me write my name in Arabic, so that he could remember me better. He said, 'Come and see me at my douar. I will have a lot of men ready to hear you.'

"Continuing my journey on foot, I arrived at Bosquet about 4.30 p.m. I was constrained to visit a Frenchman who had on my first visit looked upon me as a spy. To-day he seemed very pleased to see me. Taking me into his house he gave me grapes and biscuits to eat; he also invited me to dine with him.

"Saturday evening, I arrived at Cassaigne; here another man gave me refreshments who had sought to do me harm, saying that I was a spy, but is now very friendly. In the evening, had a meeting with the Protestants, after which I left for Bosquet, arriving there at 11 p.m., so as to avoid Sunday travelling. At Ouillis the Protestants showed me no little kindness. The meeting at this place is generally held in the schoolroom. The school-mistress was absent to-day, and had the key with her; however we descended into the ravine, and in the shade of fig and pomegranate trees had a very happy time over the Word, in prayer, and with hymns.

"Time did not allow me to visit the Arabs on Sunday. Early on Monday morning I was taken on horseback by the son of one of the Protestants to several douars. The first was that of the chief seen on Friday. Unfortunately most of the men were away at Bosquet to bury a marabout who had died on Saturday. However, those present brought out mats, and invited us to sit down. For a long time the men and a few women listened with great attention as I read from the New Testament, and spoke to them of our need of a new birth. 'Come again, and you will have all our people to hear these good words,' said the Arabs, as we rode away.

"Riding in another direction, we visited another douar. At first it seemed as though all the men were absent, threshing their wheat; however, a shepherd lad gave a shout, and soon we had a nice congregation. One man, whom I had noticed listening in great astonishment, said when I had done speaking, 'Never have I heard such things as these which you have been telling us.' Two Gospels were left with a very old 'taleb,' and a young marabout took me in his arms and embraced me when I promised to send him a Bible. Altogether I had a most encouraging time in the Dahra. I cannot go further into details, but this visit to the douars has increased my desire to be set more free from town work."

Six stations have thus been occupied within the limits of the French territory. The work has been slower of development than in Morocco, and in some respects the hindrances to the reception of the Gospel are greater; yet the establishment of settled law and order, and the liberty of conscience allowed by the Government, must prove immense advantages in the long run. In Morocco, if the hearts of the people are more ready to receive God's message of love and grace, there are terrible barriers in the way of confessing it openly. To become a Christian there is to run the risk of imprisonment, torture, and death. We must therefore rejoice that under God's overruling providence, Algeria has been brought under the influences of a civilised government.

Before passing on, mention must be made of a work begun about two years ago in the town of Algiers by Miss Trotter and two other ladies, though it is unconnected with the North Africa Mission. Hitherto these ladies have worked among the French inhabitants, trying also to reach the French-speaking Arabs, but they hope as they learn Arabic to get fuller access to the natives. The meetings held by them almost nightly have been much blessed, and although at first there was much opposition and disturbance, these are giving place to quiet attention, as their object is becoming better understood.

CHAPTER IV.

Morocco.

So I returned and considered all the oppressions that are done under the sun; and behold the tears of such as were oppressed, and they had no comforter; and on the side of their oppressors there was pow.r; but they had no comforter.—Ecclesiastes iv. 1.

HE narrowness of the strip of water which separates the empire of Morocco from Europe makes the contrast between the two countries more striking, and the fact that the starting-point for Tangier is usually Gibraltar, where English order and cleanliness prevail, enhances the effect. Scarcely three hours of crossing, and the coast line, which has been in view all the time, is reached, and the traveller sets foot in what might be a new world, so different do things appear.

The town, which is not large, is built upon sloping ground, rising up the hillside from the water, and is surrounded by a wall. The flat-roofed houses are pressed close together, intersected by labyrinths of narrow, winding streets. During the reign of our Charles I. Tangier was held by the English, and was strongly fortified, probably with the object of keeping in check the pirates who preyed upon all European vessels. In the time of Charles II. it was abandoned by England, and the fortifications destroyed. Tangier is but seldom visited by the Sultan, perhaps because it is more frequented by Europeans than any other spot in his dominions. In 1889, however, the present Sultan, Muley Hassan, honoured the town by a visit, an occasion of intense excitement and rejoicing. The city of Morocco—or, more properly, Maraksh —is the Sultan's usual abode, but he appears to move about a good deal in the interior of his dominions. The government of which he is the head and centre is described too truly as an organised system of brigandage. To squeeze money out of the unfortunate people, and bring it into the imperial coffers is the one aim and object. To be industrious and thrifty, to live in comfort,

TANGIER.

marks a man out as a suitable victim, and sooner or later some false accusation is brought against him, and he is thrown into prison, and kept there till all his possessions have been given up as bribes to buy back his liberty. The mode of collecting ordinary taxes is thus described by an old traveller, and the description may still serve for the present time, except that the word "Kaid" must be substituted for the old English term "bashaw."

"The mode practised by the Emperor for extracting money from his subjects is very simple and expeditious. He sends orders to the bashaw, or governor of the province, to pay him the sum he wants within a limited time. The bashaw immediately collects it, and sometimes double the sum, as a reward to his own industry, from the Kaids of the towns and Sheikhs of the encampments in the province which he commands. The example of the bashaw is not lost upon these officers, who take care to compensate their own trouble with equal liberality from the pockets of the subjects, so that by means of this chain of despotism, which descends from the Emperor to the meanest officer, the wretched people generally pay about four times the taxes which the Emperor receives."*

The consequence of these oppressive taxes, and still more oppressive acts of spoliation, is that the rich and fertile country is but poorly cultivated, and yields no more than will keep its population above starvation. Large tracts are covered with the palmetto, a dwarf palm resembling a fern, the fibre of which is used to weave a coarse material for the tents of the wandering Arabs. In other places the rich soil is carpeted with a profusion of wild flowers. Acres of bright yellow marigolds contrast with acres of scarlet poppies; but more commonly they are intermingled and sprinkled with the added hues of white, pink, and blue of many lovely flowers. Near the towns and villages there are, indeed, gardens where fruit and vegetables grow luxuriantly; but these serve to show what might be made of a country so rich in natural resources if it were justly governed.

The Moorish prisons are awful proofs of what the Government is, the poor creatures who are consigned to them being frequently innocent of the crimes they are accused of; yet they are left to languish there, innocent and guilty alike, their case being hopeless if they have no money wherewith to buy themselves off. The following sketch by the Rev. Newman Hall of what he saw of the prison in Tangier in 1883 will bear repetition, especially as

* Lempriere. 1813.

it is to be feared that no improvement in the state of things has taken place since then, except a little at Tangier, where European influence is felt.

"I had heard," he says, "that a small piece of black bread, insufficient to maintain life, is alone allowed, and *no water;* that charges are trumped up for the sake of extracting money; that those who can pay are released, and the penniless and friendless die, and that the Governor reckons the prisons as a source of revenue, and not of expense. I resolved to see for myself, and went in the afternoon with my Moor and a man bearing as many loaves as he could carry. There was no difficulty in getting access to the entrance-hall, where the gaoler abides. In the wall is a round hole, about a foot in diameter, through which I looked into a sort of den, with two grated openings in the roof. Here about thirty men were confined. Through a similar opening I looked into what may have been the ground-floor of a house, with a small court in the centre with recesses. Here were about sixty men promiscuously herded together. Some were lying or sitting on the stone floor, the ankles of several being chained together. The odour through the opening rendered it difficult to look long enough for the eye to get accustomed to the darkness so as to see distinctly.

"But enough, and more than enough was witnessed! I shall not soon forget the haggard hungry looks of those near the opening, nor the eager clutching hands that grasped the bread. True enough they have no water. The prisoners may buy it through the gaoler, or receive it from their friends, while those who have neither money nor friends depend on the few drops others may spare them; and it may happen sometimes that none at all reaches them. There was no well or cistern in the upper part of the town where the gaol is, so we descended to the market-place, but trade was over for the day, and the water-skin carriers had gone. An hour elapsed before we found three men with water-barrels, who for a few pence climbed the steep path to the gaol. The gaoler unlocked a small door by which the barrels were passed in. The gurgling of the water as it was emptied, mingled with the grateful murmur of the prisoners and the dismal clanking of their chains.

"Next morning another supply of bread was taken, and eight men carrying skins of water. These eight men were satisfied with a fraction more than one penny each; yet to save so small a cost so great a cruelty is inflicted! It was delightful to see some of the men availing themselves of this supply to indulge in the rare luxury of a wash. The gratitude of the poor creatures for so small a gift was distressing. One said to my guide, 'People bring us food, but they seldom think of the water.' My guide told me that there are sometimes twice as many prisoners, and that in summer the stench is intolerable. If any of them are sick, no doctor visits them, and no extra food or medicine is given. No wonder deaths are frequent!"

If such a state of things is carried on with the knowledge, and almost under the eyes of the ambassadors of Christian nations in Tangier, we may well believe that in the remote towns they are no better.

Even now the inner parts of Morocco are but little known to the civilised

CALL TO PRAYER.

world, and the dislike of the Government to letting in any light upon its darkness combines with the prejudices and fanaticism of the people to keep out all strangers. Quite recently Mr. Joseph Thomson, with a fellow traveller, forced his way, at frequent risk of being killed, through a part of the Atlas Mountains, and, though we cannot hope for any good result to the country visited by such attempts, however courageous, yet we do expect that the patient, loving attempts made by our missionary brethren and sisters to carry the healing balm of the Gospel of Jesus Christ wherever it is possible for them to go, will gradually open a way for them, even to parts that are now altogether closed. The mountain tribes of Riffs, Shluhs, and, further south, of Sus, are always spoken of by the Moors of the coast towns as wild brigands and robbers, and it is true that they are little controlled by the Sultan, and do what is right in their own eyes; but they too are among those for whom Christ died, and in them also the great Creator has implanted hearts capable of being reached by love and kindness. In many respects, so far as Mr. Thomson's observation reached, these mountaineers in their remote villages are much less debased than the strict Moslems of the plains. The picture he gives of Mahomedanism, as seen in Morocco, is a terrible one.

"It was difficult to grasp the fact which had been gradually boring its way into our minds with growing knowledge of Moorish life, that absolutely the most religious nation on the face of the earth was also the most grossly immoral. In no sect is faith so absolutely paramount, so unweakened by any strain of scepticism, as among the Mahomedans of Morocco. Among no people are prayers so commonly heard, or religious duties more rigidly attended to. Yet side by side with it all, rapine and murder, mendacity of the most advanced type, and brutish and nameless vices exist to an extraordinary degree. From the Sultan down to the loathsome, half-starved beggar, from the most learned to the most illiterate, from the man who enjoys the reputation of utmost sanctity to his openly infamous opposite, all are alike morally rotten. Everywhere Moorish misgovernment is casting its blighting influence on the brave, industrious villagers of the Atlas Mountains. Up every glen this huge, blood-sucking octopus is pushing its horrible feelers, instinct with the lust of power, dragging village after village to feed with its life-blood the rapacious appetite of this bloated monster. In some places the old independence is maintained, and there, though almost starved into submission, the Shluh fight desperately for home and freedom."

Soon may the freedom which the Son of God alone can give be brought to them.

CHAPTER V.

Morocco—Work in Tangier.

Allah akbar!—God is great!
—Old Moorish battle-cry.

The Lord of Hosts is with us.
—Psalm xlvi.

THE mission in Algeria had not long been started, before a call came to extend its operations to Morocco. As has been mentioned already, Mr. Mackintosh had become interested some years before in Moors whom he had met, away from their own country. Though himself taking up the work of the Bible Society, he was anxious that other forms of missionary effort should also be attempted. *At the same time it was brought to the notice of Mr. Glenny that a large house built by an English gentleman for his own use just outside of Tangier was for sale below cost price, and in many respects it seemed very suitable as a centre where missionaries might reside for a time while studying Arabic, before going forth to different spheres of labour. Through the kind help of a few Christian friends, the house was bought, and named Hope House, and from it for the last six years have been going forth continual loving efforts to enlighten and to win all within reach. Moors, Jews, Riffs, Spaniards, all find a welcome at Hope House, and, so far as human efforts can bring it to them, healing both for body and soul.

The first to take possession of Hope House was Mr. Baldwin, an American pastor, with his wife and family. Mrs. Baldwin soon found her hands full of work in dispensing medicine to the many patients who came to

---

* The Christian lady, Mrs. Johnson, with whom the thought of occupying Hope House as a missionary centre originated, and who gave largely towards the purchase-money, died almost immediately after it was occupied.

her for help. With her young children to care for, the work was beyond her strength, and she gladly handed it over to an English medical man, Dr. Churcher, who joined the Mission party a year or two later. The medical mission has since greatly developed. Some out-buildings attached to the house have been altered so as to make a comfortable little hospital, with room for twenty or thirty patients, enabling the doctor to take in serious cases requiring good nursing. A trained nurse, and two ladies who have acquired the needful knowledge through much practice in Tangier, find abundance of work in helping the doctor with the out-patients, and in caring for those whom they take in. To the dispensary at Hope House has been added one in the town itself, where medical help is dealt out once or twice a week. This department of Christian effort gives great opportunities for preaching the Gospel. That is done systematically to all who come for treatment, but besides the addresses given to all when assembled, the ladies of the Mission find time for quiet talks and readings with those who come, which are most helpful in breaking down prejudice and winning a hearing for the Gospel.

But from the commencement of the mission in Morocco, the freedom of access to the people, and their readiness to hear has been so great that our friends have felt limited only by their own want of language, and as that was gradually acquired, by lack of time and strength to do all that might be done. Near to Hope House is an open space, called the Marshan, and here are frequently encamped Moorish soldiers, embassies, bearers of petitions from distant parts of the country, etc., thus bringing many from distant places almost up to the doors of the Mission House. In April, 1885, Mr. Baldwin thus describes such an encampment:—

"As I write, a Moor from Fez is looking on. He is one of the officers of a large party sent from the Sultan to escort a French ambassador to Fez, and carry to the Sultan a present from the French Government. They are encamped on the Marshan, fifteen tents, and about one hundred and fifty horses and mules. I have just called on the Kaid in charge—a man of rank among those about the Sultan. I gave him my card, with my name and vocation written thereon in Arabic. He received me pleasantly. The day following he returned my visit, accompanied by two of his officers and a servant. I gave each of them a Gospel, to the Kaid I had sent a New Testament as a gift. The Moorish doctor of the expedition has since come to ask for a Gospel. The Kaid and his attendants were here nearly an hour. I spoke to him a little of the Lord Jesus, having the gardener as an interpreter.

"Oh! that we might tell them as we desire ot the great salvation. We are daily filled with thanksgiving at the most evident and multiplying openings for toil for Jesus right at our doors. The next day (Sunday) twelve chief men from the Marshan encampment came to our house, and we held a service for them under our front porch. I spoke, and Miss Herdman interpreted for me. My subject was Jesus' words to Nicodemus. They are fine intelligent men, and there was great and quiet attention to the Word. Afterwards I showed them the grounds, and gave them tea and biscuits.

"*April* 20*th*.—I was called from writing to see two of the Kaid's officers, who had again called at our house. They have given me their names and addresses, and assure me they will do all in their power for us, if we will any of us go to their country. They live at Mequinez, a little west of Fez. They say it is a beautiful and healthy city in the mountains, built with more space about the houses than at Tangier, and four times as large. Thus in God's providence we are forming valuable acquaintances in the interior, which may be of great use some day.

"*April* 23*rd*.—We are having natives about us continually, and it is hardly necessary to go outside our gate to get hold of them for conversation. Many were here yesterday, a continuous stream from morning till night. There were Riffians, Moors from this neighbourhood and the interior, with three or four Jews as well. Many of them came for and received medical treatment and medicine."

In the beginning of 1885 the mission was strengthened by the addition of two ladies, Miss Tulloch and Miss Herdman. Miss Tulloch went with the object of helping in the education of Mr. Baldwin's children, but her heart was drawn out to the people around her, and her spare time was all devoted to learning Arabic, in which she made unusually rapid progress. She little knew how short a working day in Africa was before her, but the Lord knew, and doubtless helped His servant quickly into work, and let fall some handfuls of purpose, that she might glean them. Before many months had passed, her journals show that she was able to take her share in telling out the Gospel in Arabic, though doubtless it was with stammering lips and many longings for a fuller use of language. The following extract from Miss Tulloch's journal, written August, 1885, gives a glimpse of the village work round Tangier, which is often a pleasant refreshment to weary workers:—

"*Aug.* 1*st*.—We left early this morning for the village of Beni Makadda. An hour and a half's ride brought us there. It is a large one, and built—as many of these villages are—on the crest of a hill. Being directed to a certain house, we were most kindly welcomed, for no sooner did they see us coming than they brought out nice mats and spread them under some fig trees, which gave us delightful shade. We were soon surrounded by men and children.

"We rejoiced in going forth this morning, as we had leaflets to give away, a portion of God's Word in Moorish Arabic. Those who could read were delighted with them. They listened attentively while Miss Herdman explained them to them, and told them of the need of a Saviour. When they saw us prepare for lunch, they all very politely left us, and a woman brought us milk, water, and eggs. After lunch the men came back, and many passages from the Old and New Testaments were read to them and explained. The women were afterwards visited. One woman, whom I had met going to fetch water, and had persuaded to join the group, sat and listened with rapt attention to the story of the Saviour's love, and when Miss Herdman stopped she begged her to go on. It was with difficulty we got away from her.

"*Aug. 4th.*—Read the leaflet to some men, also John iii. They gladly took the leaflet away with them. One case was most interesting, that of a taleb, or schoolmaster, who had come simply to pay a visit. I gave him a leaflet, which he read. When he came to where it speaks of the Son of man being lifted up, he asked, like the eunuch of old, 'Of whom is this spoken?' I told him it was of the Lord Jesus, and as best I could explained to him the need of His death. Then he said, 'I will read it over again,' which he did, and pondered over each sentence to take it in. I then brought him an Arabic Bible, and opened Genesis for him, the Moslems being always ready to read that book; but with wistful eyes he said, 'Show me the Gospel; I want to

MISS TULLOCH.

read about the Lord Jesus.' I turned up John iii. quickly, but when he saw it he said, sorrowfully, 'I cannot read that! I am only a poor taleb; you know more than I do.' I got John iii., which we have now written out in Moorish Arabic, and he read the whole chapter. When he left he said he would soon come again.

"*Aug.* 24*th*.—In going among the patients to-day, a woman, for the first time, asked me to read to her the leaflet; I had given her one. I did so, and tried to speak to her and those beside her of the Lord Jesus. Two listened attentively. The woman who asked me to read begged for another leaflet, that she might give it to her son.

"Went in the morning to the Sok (market). The gathering was immense; I had never seen it so full. There were thousands present; it seemed as if there was not even standing room. Some men asked me for something to read. I did not stay long, but went to ask after a sick woman, and was glad to find her better. Had a long talk with a young wife in the same house about the Lord Jesus, and heard from her of the death of a girl who had been their servant, and had but lately left them. Being a country girl (or from the mountains, as they say), she did not know how to sew as the town girls do. She was pleased to learn, and I used to teach her, and while she sewed I talked to her of the Lord Jesus. The last time I called to see her, I found her mother had come to take her home. I was sorry I had lost my pupil Fatima. To-day I was told she was killed on the way home—shot by her brother. 'That is the way the Moslems do,' added the young woman who told me. Poor Fatima! How we must use each opportunity we have of speaking, as if it were to be the last and only one."

Rather less than two years was the time granted to Miss Tulloch thus to use the opportunities given her. She went to Tangier the beginning of 1885, and in December, 1886, an attack of typhoid fever laid her low. It was the messenger sent to take her home, for in spite of the most careful and loving nursing she did not rally. But before her short working day came to a close she was permitted to rejoice over two souls from among the Moslems, whom she believed to be born again of the Spirit. One was a poor old man from Fez, who came seeking medical help for a bad sore on his chest. Having made the pilgrimage to Mecca, he went by the name of El Haj, the pilgrim. His coming to Tangier was before the days of the present convenient little hospital, but he settled himself down in a corner of the stable, and was allowed to remain, and accepted as the first "in-patient." Many prayers went up for him from loving hearts that, as God had sent him, he might receive healing of both body and soul. Both prayers were, so far as human insight could go, graciously answered. His bodily health was quite restored, and during the weeks spent at the Mission-house he drank in the Gospel message brought to him chiefly by Miss Tulloch. He used to go about singing to himself, "Jesus loves me, this I know," in Arabic, and he was not afraid to speak boldly before the others of the Lord Jesus being his Saviour. When his cure was complete he went back to his own place, but Miss Tulloch fully expected to meet him again in heaven.

The other case was that of a young man of good birth and education, who came to visit the missionaries, and was so attracted by what he saw and heard that he stayed on for some time. Miss Tulloch set him to translate the Psalms into Moorish Arabic, which Mohamedans like, although they know little of them; then she would read what he had written as her lesson. Thus they went right through the Psalms together, which filled him with a great desire to pray, and he learnt many short prayers. He also read Matthew with a class of the whole mission-party, and Miss Tulloch and he began to translate the Epistles into Moorish Arabic. They had many interesting conversations as they read together daily, and the truth took hold of him. One day he read the Epistle of John by himself.

Miss Tulloch says :—

"I had shown him the first chapter, seventh verse, and then I believe he gave himself to Jesus. That night he wept in his bed, and he felt as if the Lord Jesus came to him, and he said, 'O Lord, here is my heart—take it!' He was so bright the next morning, and so happy. He wrote to his parents that he was going to follow the Lord Jesus, for His religion was better than theirs. They replied that he was no son of theirs, and that they would put him in prison if he came home."

This young man was enticed home on a false pretext of his mother's illness. He was kept a prisoner, and greatly persecuted for several weeks, but has since returned to the Mission and been baptised. His return was not till after Miss Tulloch's death. When he was going away he said to her, "You may know that, if I die, I die in the religion of Sidna Aissa," and she wrote, "I cannot tell you how glad I am about his being a Christian. It is so encouraging to go on working."

Now the sickle is laid down, but the fruits remain.

Almost at the same time with Miss Tulloch, in the early part of 1885, Miss Herdman joined the party at Hope House. She had the great advantage of some previous knowledge of Arabic, as well as Spanish, and both languages were speedily brought into active use. A busy year was spent in interpreting for the doctor as he treated his patients, as well as for the other missionaries, in visiting the houses of both Moors and Jews, and, among other varied pieces of work, putting some of the familiar Sankey's hymns into Moorish Arabic, which last has been an invaluable help in teaching the Gospel. Then there came a call for an onward step, the history of which will be given in the next chapter.

CHAPTER VI.

ARZILA AND LARACHE.

The fields are all ripening, and far and wide,
The world now is waiting the harvest-tide ;
But reapers are few, and the work is great,
And much will be lost should the harvest wait.

ARZILA.

IN the spring of 1886, several Christian visitors were attracted to Hope House; among others, Mr. Hind Smith, the well-known secretary of the Young Men's Christian Association, and his son. In order to see as much of the country as possible, these two gentlemen made a journey of a few days into the interior, in company with Mr. Baldwin, returning by the western coast. Their way led them by Arzila, an ancient walled city, washed by the Atlantic, about thirty miles S.W. of Tangier, and containing 2,000 inhabitants. Mr. Baldwin wrote :—

"I shall never forget standing, with Mr. Hind Smith, on the crumbling walls of Arzila, at its south-west corner. The sun was just sinking into the sea, amid a blaze of glory cast on cloud and wave. About us was a group of lads who followed us everywhere, and with whom we had been speaking. The lads of this quiet, ancient town are unusually intelligent and interesting, most of them being able to read Arabic. Standing there we prayed for the lost ones about us."

Mr. Hind Smith was so interested and stirred by the sight, that he offered to pay the rent of a house in the town for a year, if it could be occupied by some of the mission workers. On their return to Tangier, it was at once arranged that Miss Herdman should go there, taking as her companion Miss Constance Caley, who had then not been long in the country, and knew but little of the language, but who rapidly acquired it. Like Miss Tulloch, she was to have but a few brief years filled with earnest work for the Master, before she also was taken home to rest.

Thirty miles is the distance between Arzila and Tangier, and thirty miles does not seem much on paper, and with English notions of travel, but to them it meant a long day's journey on mules through a roadless country, with two rivers to ford and rocky hills to climb.

In a small Moorish house of two rooms, with no glass windows, and furniture of the scantiest, consisting chiefly of boxes turned upside down to form seats and tables, these two dear sisters made themselves at home. They were the only European inhabitants of the place, surrounded by Jews and Moslems. A Jew acted as a kind of Consul for all nations, England included, but he could not speak English. He was, however, kind and friendly, as were all their neighbours.

There was no need to go in search of work. A constant stream of visitors came to them, so that often it was difficult to secure time for meals and needful quiet. The more educated men, both Moors and Jews, delighted in coming to read and converse. Miss Herdman had to try to keep them to separate hours, as they required different instruction, and different lines of truth to be brought before them. Many of the Jews spoke Spanish, the Moslems Arabic. The women came in groups, and listened gladly to the Gospel story, Miss Herdman turning it into Moorish Arabic as she read. The boys had their special hour, generally forming a sort of body-guard to the ladies, and accompanying them in their evening stroll on the sands, or round the once strong, but now decaying walls. At the end of a month Miss Herdman wrote:

"A month of unspeakable mercy ends. Miss Caley and I both feel that we have indeed been privileged to have been sent here. These people are willing to hear, and one brings another and says to us, 'I told him (or her) you would tell them about God out of your books,' and in several instances in visiting women who have not been to our house they say, 'Now read to us,' or, 'Now tell us about Jesus,' of their own accord."

Miss Caley's slight knowledge of medicine soon developed into greater skill by abundant practice, as there were constant calls for help to the sick, and even for the treatment of gunshot wounds, but so great was the readiness to hear in Arzila among all classes that the medical work was hardly needed as a means for removing prejudices and making people willing to listen as in other places.

"Quite early went to see a young woman, who we feared was dying, but had the joy of seeing her greatly relieved by our treatment, in answer to prayer, and heartfelt hallelujahs rose to God. Several came afterwards for medicine; among them one who, a month ago, was a poor, miserable, dirty, sick woman; she came many days to have a bad sore dressed, and to-day we hardly knew her, she looked so clean and tidy; she is now well and has a much brighter expression. We trust she has learnt that there is One in Heaven who loves her, and some on earth who care for her.

"Then a man came to ask if we would go to a collection of huts a little way out of the town, to see a man who had been stabbed four nights ago, and was in great pain. We sent for donkeys at once, but there is always much delay in this country; however, after sending again and again they came in about two hours, and then one of them had not a vestige of a bridle! We could not find our 'big man,' who always accompanies us, so started with the man who came to tell us, and the son of our servant. It has been a lovely day, and we much enjoyed our ride. It was a great pleasure to get outside the walls into the fresh country air. In about an hour we reached the hut to which we were bound, and found the poor man lying on a piece of matting, groaning and looking very miserable. The stab, made either with a sword or a large knife, was in the thigh, near the hip-joint, but, as far as I could tell, had only injured the flesh. I soon strapped it up, gave him medicine, and trust that in five or six days he will be all right. The people from the other huts gathered, and soon thirteen were listening while we sang and talked to him of sin and the Saviour. Not one in the hamlet could read, so it was of no use leaving our Scripture leaflets. When we left, we were presented with a chicken and two large melons, and the patient said that when he is well, he will come and see us, ' en shah Allah' (if God will).

"Just before reaching the huts, our 'big man' came up with us. On our homeward journey, he told us that the man who had been our companion and guide going, was the would-be murderer. He had come for us because he had feared the man would die, and then he would have been imprisoned; if the injured man lives, no notice will be taken of his dreadful deed. We thought he was rather a surly man, but spoke and sang to him as we rode along, so he has heard the Gospel message. We passed near the place where an attempt was made on some men's lives last July, but God has delivered us from fear, for 'greater is He that is in us than he that is in the world,' and 'if God be for us, who can be against us?'

"Visited a very nice Sherifa, quite a dignified lady, widow of a Kaid. She and the friends with her were all very attentive to the Word of God, and our singing and expounding. These Sherifas, who are descendants of Mohammed, never even visit one another, but, having large gardens, go out with a friend or two and spend a few hours in them often now in summer, hurrying out of the city gate closely covered. They are always glad to see us, as their life is monotonous.

"The Sherifas we visited yesterday sent to beg us to come again, and made us breakfast with them. Again read, sung, and spoke of Jesus, as we do in every house, at every visit.

"Visited Moorish and Jewish houses, one of the Moorish being our neighbour's, the head Sherif of Arzila and Alcazar.

"The Sherifa had her afternoon tea-party, for Friday is the visiting day of the Moorish ladies, and we joined the circle. Slaves were sitting behind spinning wool with a distaff. Each house makes its own clothing, or rather they prepare the wool for it. Too much conversation to read, but sang and explained the words.

"*Saturday.*—Spent a happy day. At half-past eight the Jewesses began to come. We had Jews in to-day from the Riff country, Alcazar and Laraches, as well as those of Arzila. We devote Saturday to them. About five, after receiving Jews all day, we went for a walk on the hard sands, the tide being out, begging the boys not to follow us, as our voices were tired. However, on our return, we had our usual congregation of Moors and Jews on the sands, and afterwards as we were going home, two Moors following us at a respectful distance, we could not find it in our hearts not to ask them in. One, a scribe, begged for an Arabic Testament to copy. They had tea with us, and were much interested."

As time went on, Miss Herdman and Miss Caley began to see increased understanding of their message, and receptiveness on the part of many. In some they had reason to think that the Spirit of God was really working, and especially this was the case with two men and a woman, whom they attended in sickness, and who passed away trusting in the Lord Jesus Christ.

"A Mooress came for medicine for her dying husband to ease his agony. Seeing us busy, she said, ' My husband wants you *so* much to come and speak to him of the Lord Jesus, but perhaps you cannot come to-day.' The house being cleared, I went out in the rain, the streets being only passable at each side, where they slope for a few inches. The man professes faith in the Lord Jesus Christ. I always pray with the household, and, to-day, I felt that he was praying too in the Holy Ghost. He told me three or four days ago, and has since, that his sins were gone, washed in the blood of the Lord Jesus Christ. He held my hand and said, ' Don't go ; stay all night,' for it was then dark. So I promised (God willing) to come early to-morrow. I could not make out all he said, so he said to his wife, 'Tell her to talk to me, I like to hear, and I understand it all, but am too weak to answer.'"

The dying man held in his hand the Wordless Book, which had been used on former visits to explain to him the way of salvation. Miss Herdman seeing it in his hand, turned over to the last page, where the gilded leaf tries to suggest the thought of the coming glory which she saw he was nearing, but he turned it back to the red, saying, "This is what I am clinging to—the blood of Jesus."

"The Moor died an hour after I left on Thursday. We are comforted to know that he is for ever with the Lord. I have made inquiries concerning him, and am told he was honest, truthful, humble-minded, and devout—one whose heart was prepared for the good seed, so that it fell on good ground.

"We paid a very satisfactory visit yesterday to a house, where one whom we have often visited is, we believe, saved. Her eyes brighten at the name of Jesus, and, weak and ill as she was yesterday, she sang, not the chorus only, but every word she could follow in the hymns. This woman teaches her little boy our hymns, and they both sing ere they sleep at night (in Arabic, of course) 'Jesus loves me, this I know.'

"To-day an elderly woman who knew the Lord Jesus Christ was gathered home. Her sister told me every one observed what a sweet smile she had on her face after death. This is the third of the Lord's people here who has gone home. Another, we fear, will die. I felt much rejoiced to-day while reading God's Word with him. He grows in grace daily. He fasted yesterday, to spend the day in seeking for more of the Lord Jesus, and in praying for Jews and Moors. He teaches his wife every evening, and he says he believes the truth is entering her heart.

"We visited a house where we got a hearty welcome, and a request to sing, 'for,' said the mistress of the house, 'my boy knows all your hymns and sings them to us, and your religion is beautiful.' After singing and reading passages of Scripture, and some conversation, we invited them to our house. 'Yes,' said the mother, 'we will come, for what you say enters my heart, and I want to come and get it cleansed.'"

The work was increasing in interest, and many heart-ties had been formed between our sisters and the people of Arzila, but during the second year of their stay there Miss Herdman's health frequently failed. Several times she was obliged to leave for a few weeks to seek restoration, but always, on going back, the symptoms returned. It seemed clear that she could not remain there, at any rate during the summer, and Larache was fixed on as a place easy of access, and which might perhaps prove more healthy. From thence, also, they hoped to be able to pay occasional visits to Arzila, as the distance was only twenty-two miles, and the road for most of the way easy, along the sea-beach. Miss Caley, after a visit to Arzila, brought back cheering news.

"The fokee who died since we left Arzila rested his dying head on the large New Testament and Psalms I had given him, and refused to let it be touched, saying to those around him, 'I die, trusting in Jesus Christ and His precious word.'

"Another Arzila man, very talented, although not a fluent reader (being a merchant, not a fokee), went to Tangier to look for us, and gave clear testimony at Hope House of his faith in the Lord Jesus Christ, before other Arzila men. He has been quietly teaching the Gospel for months since he learned it from us. We are greatly encouraged by this. Our Hope House friends asked, Did he keep the Mohammedan fast of Ramadan? and he replied that had he not done so he would have been cruelly beaten, as a sick boy in Arzila was treated, but that when there were more converts they would dare to come out boldly.

"I went to see some of our special friends. One was very ill, and as I said, 'Perhaps you will not get better,' she answered at once, 'Then I'll go to be with the Lord Jesus, the beloved One, the Saviour, because of His precious blood,' and she and her sister both repeated some of the texts we had taught them before we left, now nearly four months ago."

At Larache Miss Herdman and Miss Caley found abundance of open doors and work to be done of the same kind as at Arzila, although they did not form so many close friendships. In addition to the work among Moors and Jews, their house was open to the Spanish and Portuguese sailors who frequently came there. The port of Larache is rendered dangerous by a sand bar, which has accumulated across the mouth of the river, but it is still frequented by small steamers and other vessels, which come for oranges in the season, and for cargoes of canary seed and other produce. The sailors were usually delighted with the hymn-singing in their own tongue—Miss Herdman having procured hymn-books from Lisbon and Madrid in both languages—and with the simple Gospel told to them, and tracts and Gospels given to them to take away.

In June, 1887, some of the mission party from Hope House visited Larache, and it was arranged that Miss Herdman and Miss Caley should accompany Mr. and Miss Baldwin on a short tour southwards. The following are some notes of the journey:—

"MAZAGAN.—While marketing this morning, Miss Baldwin and I had again large audiences. One fokee sent for us, and after seating us, asked us to speak about the books I had with me. We have met with great politeness from the people here, and many of them have at least heard, and intelligently understood, the way of salvation. The population is somewhere between 15,000 and 20,000.

"Yesterday Miss Baldwin and I visited a Sheikh's family. Passing through three courts open to the public we then entered a private and very large one, with three rooms and a kitchen taking up three sides of it. We were shown into the longest room I have seen in this country. A few women were reclining, hungry and thirsty, and pale, poor things, from the severe fast of Ramadan, bad at all times, but especially trying in June, when the day during which they must neither eat nor drink is both long and hot. We rather sigh for cold water sometimes, but feel ashamed of ourselves, seeing them so patiently bear thirst. We hardly ever dare take water, it being often very dirty, drinking tea and coffee instead. A large proportion of the wells are brackish too, and spoil the tea, and do not quench thirst. We are only separated by sand banks and dunes on all this coast road from the ocean.

MISS CALEY.

"A number of women and children, both white and slaves, soon joined us. They asked us a few questions, and we read, and sang, and spoke to them of Jesus. We found that the families of three brothers, fokees, occupied different rooms in the same house. I gave medicine for malarial fever to a very young wife, and a penny looking-glass to another, and on returning to our tent a present of a fowl and eggs was sent to us. They made us Moorish tea with plenty of mint in it. Some of the women would not allow that any one but Mohammed could save, some were indifferent; one asked many intelligent questions, and made the children keep quiet, that she might hear.

"On Monday evening we stopped on the slope of a hill close to a douar, or village of tents. We conversed with the villagers, especially speaking to them of their sin. When all had left us at dusk, not one able to read, a taleb from another village came up and listened, and begged for a book. I gave him a New Testament. He said, 'These words of the Lord Jesus enter into the heart.'

"It is very dangerous for Moors to be out after dark in these parts, but as death is the punishment for killing a Christian we are in less danger,

When a Moorish traveller is missing, a few of the inhabitants of the douars through which he passed are thrown into prison, but on their paying an indemnity to the Government they are all released, and but rarely the man who committed the deed is kept long in prison, unless he has no friends; then he dies of starvation. So murder is common, not being more severely punished than theft. Our hearts are saddened by such people as these saying, 'We murder, we are robbers, we steal, our lives are evil; but no matter, we shall all go to heaven; our Lord Mohammed will intercede for us after death with God.' I believe God is blessing us on this trip to teach some that they must be born again. In heathen lands we expect such open sin, but certainly we are surprised to find Mohammedans as degraded as savages, and far more bloodthirsty than some savage tribes.

"Encamped on a lovely spot on the sands. There is what is rare on this coast, a little bay, but so full of rocks it would not do even for a fishing harbour. Last night we spent outside one of the Government fundaks, although, as usual, urgently entreated to enter, being told that close to where we put our tents murdered persons were interred under the heaps of stones, as well as in a little river we had just crossed. We sent in the mules to be safe from robbers, and stayed outside enjoying a cool sea-breeze, while within was the customary dunghill. The place has a very ill name, but we let our men sleep, and had neither soldier nor guard, trusting in the Lord. We had conversation with groups last night and this morning, and feel the sin of this land more and more laid upon our hearts as a burden, until the Lord works mightily, giving repentance unto life.

"*Sunday*.—Encamped outside another fundak with the usual warnings. The people are kind, and brought us provisions last night, and have been with us off and on all day. A taleb—one of the two who can read—from the tents near, is now sitting with me. He says he teaches the people to pray, and fast, and give alms, but they all lie and steal. I said, 'Of course, because you do,' and he answered, 'Our religion is broad, yours is narrow. Those who *keep* your faith like you, do not lie, or steal, or live bad lives, but in our religion we may do all that, and go to heaven, if only we believe in God and Mohammed.'

"Have been meditating on the work there is to do among the wild Arabs, independently from that among the civilised dwellers in towns. The dwellers in towns are few; the mass of the people are wild and wicked, with just enough of Mohammedanism to lead them straight to hell. Yesterday in the village as we spoke to a large tentful, and in the field, or near our tents, as we talked they said, 'It is true; you keep your religion and do not lie or steal or lead bad lives, yet for all that we who do these things are sure of heaven through the intercession of Mohammed. You should by rights have your throats cut by us, and you will all go to hell.' And yet we felt that they were learning, and that God did not send us in vain. The moral condition of these hamlets of tents is little, if any, above that of the heathen. We have felt privileged to go among them, and long, as the Lord opens the way, to get more and more into the interior, to make known the way of truth and holiness, without which

INTERIOR OF MOSQUE OF BOU-MEDINE.

no man shall see the Lord. Our hearts bleed to see a nation going down to hell, for they are without repentance. We give ourselves unto prayer.

"Spent the afternoon evangelizing in Salee, the pirate city. We gathered groups of men and boys in various places, and walked the length and breadth of the city. Arrived back quite tired, after walking in Rabat and Salee nearly all day in the heat. We had audiences in Rabat in the morning, when we spoke of righteousness and judgment to come, as well as of Jesus and His precious blood.

"Salee contains from 15,000 to 20,000 inhabitants. Nearly all its streets have side paths, and are laid out regularly, those on either side of the main thoroughfare being streets of private houses. There are fine old gates in partial ruins, and walls well preserved round the city, and again round the suburbs, which are full of gardens, well-watered, and abounding in a great variety of fruits. Mulberries, pears, plums and early figs are in season now. Outside the walls there are gardens with thousands of orange and lemon trees, and vineyards extend for a mile or so in every direction. On one side is the sea, on the other the sands leading down to the river. On the highest point of the city is a fine old mosque, so that Salee is beautiful for situation."

But we must not continue the journal, though it is full of interest. Salee is memorable as being a nest of pirates, the famous "Salee Rovers," in the old days of Moslem power. It is built on one side of the mouth of a river where it enters the Atlantic, Rabat being built on the opposite side.

Dr. Kerr, a medical missionary sent by the English Presbyterians, with his wife, were stationed at Rabat at the time of our friends' visit, and with them they had much happy intercourse, and received from Dr. and Mrs. Kerr much kindness.

Miss Herdman and Miss Caley returned to Larache, and worked on there with occasional visits to Arzila, until the spring of 1888.

Miss Herdman's interest had long been attracted to Fez. Mr. Baldwin had visited it in 1886, and his visit had not been without blessing, but his knowledge of Arabic was then small, and he had not been able to stay long. Miss Herdman longed to go and see for herself what openings for work were there. The people from Fez, whom she had met, had seemed to her particularly intelligent and friendly, and, from all she could hear, that city appeared to her more worthy of being the capital of the country than Morocco itself. It is the largest city of the Empire of Morocco, and is situated in the heart of the country to the west of the Atlas Mountains, which are not so high there as further south. Its distance from Tangier in a straight line is not more than 115 miles, and only 100 miles from the Atlantic coast, but the journey there on mules occupies five or six days. In April, 1888, Miss Herdman started from Larache, accompanied by Miss Caley and two other ladies, probably the first ladies who had ever attempted to visit the old Moorish city.

"*April* 19*th*.—We are encamped on a breezy hill with an extensive view of wild country, on which are a few villages of huts like the one near which our tent is pitched. In the back ground, to the east, towards Alcazar and Wazan, and to the north-east towards Tetuan, are high mountains. Praise the Lord, we have had a pleasant journey since we left Larache this morning, not however without incidents. Several persons are with us, travelling at their own expense for our protection. One of our muleteers being a soldier, we are able without extra expense to conform to the Government regulation which requires us to take one.

"We are now going to rest in this large village, after having preached the Gospel to friendly and attentive groups of men and women, and Miss Caley has given medicine to thirteen persons by moonlight. She seeks to administer medicine to body and soul to each individual.

"20*th*.—Rising a little after 4 a.m. we were ready to receive the villagers at 6.30. Thirty-five patients were attended to by Miss Caley, while I spoke of a Saviour for them all, to the sick, and the other villagers who came around our tent. We were well received, and so was our message. One woman who was especially interested, expressed a wish to belong to the Lord Jesus. She had heard of Him through a family we had taught at Larache, and thus we get constant encouragement to persevere in making known the glad tidings of salvation. The people brought us eggs, milk and butter as a thank-offering for the medicines, so we had only to pay for the barley for our animals. At nine we started, and rode for three hours over moorlands bright with lavender, and for the rest of the day through a pretty pasture country covered with wild flowers, of which I counted yesterday and to-day ninety-four varieties. Occasionally, we had to cross lowlands where the soil—heavy clay, still wet—was most toilsome to ourselves and our laden animals, and we were very thankful to find a resting-place before sunset in the courtyard of a sheikh, in the village of Karia. We were a little startled after tea by the sudden entrance of a well-dressed Moor into our tent, who peremptorily ordered us to show our books, and then said, 'Confess your faith in Mohammed at once, or you are not welcome here.' Our men were very much distressed, but afraid to put him out, as he was the son of our host excited with drink, which Mohammedans are not supposed to indulge in. However, the Shereef, who is travelling with us at his own expense, turned out a true friend, for his position entitled him to take hold of the man by the shoulders and drag him out of the tent. One of our men said, 'I dared not have done it; he would certainly have killed me with his loaded gun.' The Lord has graciously delivered us from all nervousness, and we were not made the least uneasy by the incident.

"Early this morning we went to the house of the Sheikh; it was full of women: wives, sons' wives, slaves, etc. The Sheikh's principal wife asked us in to read, and then asked for a Gospel for her husband—willingly given. Another, I think a son's wife, offered me a peseta (ninepence-halfpenny) for one for her husband; she had also one given her. This was after she had heard our hymns, and some earnest words from Miss Caley, and asked, would she find the words in the book? She seemed to feel her need of a Saviour, and to understand what we taught her. We then went out into the open market, and had audiences of soldiers and villagers until we started. Two Gospels and a small New Testament were received by good readers who asked for books, and we set out on our journey praising the Lord for seed sown in that village. During the day we had difficulties again with rivers, ditches, and, worst of all, mud; but although our men had a few falls, there was nothing serious, and we stopped at noon to rest and eat at the best-known country market of this province. They are all called by the name of the day on which they are held; this was the 'Wednesday.' The village, nestled in prickly-pear hedges, and surrounded by a deep ditch to protect the cattle from thieves at night, is hidden from view. We visited the people in their tents, and again had good audiences and willing listeners. Just at the end, a man ordered his wife, seated on the ground outside the tent, who was asking me serious questions about sin and salvation, to jump up and leave people who did not believe in Mohammed; but public opinion was against him, and he left, and his wife said, 'Go on, tell me another little word,' an Arabic idiom for, Continue the subject.

"At last by about five we reached El Habassu, which is to be our resting place for the Sunday—quite an attractive little village, with its open roadway, round which the houses are built. We waited quietly till our men had asked permission of the Kaid to pitch our tent, and then made our way to a wild semi-orchard, semi-garden place, where were other travellers camping out and many horses. We soon pitched our tent and prepared our evening meal, and early retired to rest in preparation for a busy happy day on the morrow. The Kaid sent us a present of two fine fowls—an acceptable gift, as we had had no meat since leaving Larache.

"*Sunday.*—Several men came at 8 o'clock for medicine, and so when we had finished prayers and tidied our tent, we rolled up our mattress, and spread our cushion pillows for seats; then we opened one end of the tent, and invited our guests to sit down on the matting with us. Miss Herdman had a good talk with them about the things of God, while Miss Caley administered medicine. More and more gathered, till we had three rows of brown faces encircled by the white woollen hoods of their jalabs, or cloaks, the boys and young men sitting in the front row, others kneeling and standing behind. Miss Caley spoke to them so earnestly, and we sang to them some of our simple Gospel hymns in Arabic.

"In the afternoon I [Miss Jennings] rested and guarded the tent, while the other ladies went to the Kaid's house, for he had sent repeated invitations to us to come in the morning. They were kindly received by the ladies of his household, who gave them tea and Moorish cakes, and then they went through a court into another establishment of ladies, who also listened attentively, and then to other smaller houses, and to the prison, where are 500 prisoners.

"In the evening a great number of people came for medicine, to whom

MOSQUE IN MOROCCO.

the Gospel was preached before their bodily wants were attended to. Miss Caley treated thirty-five patients in all to-day. Our rule is not to give medicine on Sunday, but we have made what we think a lawful exception to this rule to-day, for hoping to leave early to-morrow, we feel there would be no other opportunity.

"*Monday.*—Our way led through a wild marshy land, and there were streams to cross. At a quarter to ten we came to the river Sebou, and then began a curious scene. All the animals were first taken into the large flat boat, while we waited on the bank, and Miss Caley embraced the opportunity of telling about Jesus to a poor countrywoman. At length, when all the baggage was packed up on one side, and the unladen animals fixed in the body of the boat, we were each one carried separately, sedan-chair fashion, by two of the men across the mud into the boat, and, sitting on our luggage, we—animals and all—were safely rowed to the other side, and, climbing the steep bank, took the opportunity of taking a little more breakfast and resting a few minutes while the mules were re-packed.

"A group of Moors afforded Miss Herdman the opportunity of a very earnest talk about the way to heaven, and Christ's sacrifice for sins. They at once put up the cards with which they were playing, and listened most attentively, and three of them gladly received portions of God's Word. Miss Caley meantime talked to a few poor women.

"Then we remounted, and rode on through uncounted miles of high table marsh-land, for the most part dry, and just luxuriant with wildflowers. We rested early in the afternoon among the daisies, but had only shut our eyes for ten minutes when our men called us to remount, they so wanted to press forward and get to a certain safe village, where we should have the Pasha's protection for the night, as we were then passing through the wildest, wickedest tribes of this country—the Beni Hassan. About four, our horses and mules were so done up with the long day's journey and want of water, that we determined to encamp at one of these Arab villages, but as we neared it we thought it so wild and unsafe-looking—they are murderers as well as robbers, we heard—that we encouraged each other and our tired steeds to go on. At 5.30 we felt we ought not to proceed further into this almost trackless tableland, where we could not see in the distance any sign of a respectable village, and so left the road and made our way across the pasture and wheatfields to a village of huts, taking our men's advice not to go to the people and offer them medicine, or our tent-doors would be besieged, and we knew not if they might be tempted to rob us in the night. So we, quietly riding up, to the villagers' astonishment and dislike, chose a free grassy spot inside their village, and quickly erected our tent and got all our possessions inside, and securely fastened our door, the men pitching their tent close beside ours, and soon we lighted a fire for tea, we were so hungry and thirsty. Our trust is in God, and we know He will protect us from the poor wild robbers and fierce dogs, which latter, as I write this, are barking furiously outside our canvas walls. Our men have asked the people for milk and eggs, which usually they are glad to sell us, and which make our staple food, but nothing will they let us have; however, our hunger has been satisfied with what we had with us, and we are going to bed with grateful, restful hearts."

After about two and a half days' more travelling, Fez was reached, and our sisters settled themselves into a house which was provided for them by the Governor of the city, to whom they had a letter from the Moorish Minister of Foreign Affairs, who resides at Tangier. The heat was trying in the month of May, chiefly because they were confined almost entirely to the very close atmosphere of the small Moorish house in which they lived, the rooms of which were lighted and ventilated only by apertures high up in the walls, and by the door, which opened into a small court. The Governor thought himself responsible for their safety, and gave them very strict injunctions about not going out, nor even being seen upon their house-top, where they would gladly have gone for a breath of fresh air after the heat of the day. They did, however, pay a few visits, muffled up in Moorish garments. But their time was fully occupied by the crowds of patients who came to them, and kept them busy talking, singing, and giving medicines. They stayed about three weeks, during which time 690 patients were treated, all of whom, and many more, heard the Gospel story.

The return journey, which was to Tangier instead of to Larache, was a trying one. At Mequinez, where they stopped for a few days, Miss Herdman was attacked with serious illness, so that her companions despaired of her life, but the Lord graciously restored her, and she was no sooner able to stand than she set out again, anxious that the whole party, with mules and men, should not be longer detained. Before starting, she obtained from the men a promise that they would halt whenever she asked them to do so, as she feared being pushed on beyond her strength, but the promise on which she relied was of little avail. The first day, after riding several hours, she begged them to stop at a village they had come to, but no! the men said they would all be murdered if they did so, as the villagers had their guns loaded, so the weary traveller had to ride on almost fainting. During the six days which the journey occupied, Miss Herdman was able to take nothing but milk, and often that could not be got in sufficient quantities; nevertheless, the air revived her, and she gained strength day by day till Hope House was reached, where a warm welcome and kind care awaited her and the others of the party.

Miss Herdman went to England for a few months to recruit, and then returned to take up more permanent work in Fez.

Miss Caley worked on for a short time longer in Tangier, and then, being

PASSAGE OF THE SEBOU.

engaged to be married to Dr. Churcher, she came to England in August, 1888, on a visit to her family.

She expected quickly to return to the work she so loved, but her brief working day was over. Almost immediately after reaching her home she was taken ill, and after one week of fever she entered into rest. In the midst of the happy, busy days in Arzila and Larache, and with the prospect of added earthly happiness on her marriage, there are many little sentences in her journals which show that her treasure was in heaven, and her heart there also. She had greatly won the affections of the people in Arzila, and had been the means, she believed, of leading several to a saving faith in the Lord Jesus Christ. Who can measure the joy which must be hers as she meets with one and another in the Heavenly country to whom she was privileged to point out the way which has led them to it. To have brought some first-fruits from dark Morocco unto Christ was, indeed, worth living for, and worth dying for.

CHAPTER VII.

MOROCCO.

Far, far away, in deepest darkness dwelling,
Millions of souls for ever may be lost.
Who, who will go, Salvation's story telling,
Looking to Jesus, counting not the cost?

HAVING followed Miss Herdman's and Miss Caley's special work so far, we must now look back at the workers connected with Hope House.

During the two years spent by the ladies in Arzila and Larache, several had joined the Mission party, while others, in various ways, were withdrawn from it. At the close of 1886, there was a time of severe trial from illness. Mr. Pryor, a young schoolmaster who had gone, hoping to find work in that capacity among Moslem boys, was laid down with a prolonged attack of typhoid fever, and though, by God's blessing, upon careful nursing, he at length recovered, yet it soon became evident that he would never be able for work in Tangier, and he had, reluctantly, to return to England. Miss Tulloch's illness followed, which ended in her death, and Dr. Churcher was attacked by the same disease, but crossed at once to Gibraltar, to be treated in the hospital there, and he recovered quickly. Soon after, Mr. Baldwin left with his family, to take up work in Mogador, independently of the North Africa Mission.

During the year 1887 the medical work in Tangier was largely developed. The small hospital for in-patients, combined with convenient rooms for seeing and treating out-patients, was built; or rather, what had been stables and outhouses were adapted and enlarged to meet these requirements. It was named the "Tulloch Memorial Hospital," in memory of the beloved

TETUAN.

sister who did so much for the sick during the early days of the Mission, and who was the first of the Mission band to hear the Master's call: "Enter into the joy of thy Lord."

Even before the money for the hospital had been obtained, Dr. Churcher wrote:

"During the year 1886, it has been the writer's privilege to be engaged in what he ventures to think is one of the wisest methods of Christian work, viz., a medical mission, healing for soul and body, calculated pre-eminently to remove prejudice and opposition, and prepare good ground for the sowing of the Gospel seed. Over a thousand cases have been treated during the year, medicines and advice being given free, linked together with the Bread of life—the Gospel in all simplicity, and therefore in power.

"The number of patients has not been limited for want of applicants, but in order not to crowd out spiritual work among those who are seen, the study of the language, etc., many have been sent away. Did but time, circumstances, and *funds* permit we could soon be engaged, we feel sure, all day long, attending to the sick, and speaking to them of the Lord Jesus. This branch of work has procured us friends in many parts of Morocco; our patients sometimes come from long distances, perhaps five or six days' journey; neither are they unmindful of the favours received. One of them said the other day to a lady missionary, who was giving her some medicine, 'Your religion must be good, because *you* are so good.' Besides their profuse thanks, they often bring us presents and insist on our accepting them; they are usually of small value, a few eggs, a jar of honey, or some fruit, but they indicate kindness and goodwill, which are most valuable. We cannot refuse their gifts if we would, they are so heartily given. A missionary had rendered some Moors a kindness; they brought soon after a full bag of corn as a present. In vain he remonstrated. 'It was not for a present,' said he, 'that I rendered you that service, but from love to you.' 'Yes,' they replied at once, 'and it is from love to you we bring you this.'

"It is that this *twice* blessed work may be developed, and that many Moors may receive healing for their sicknesses, but, most of all, and beyond and before everything else, may be born again into the Kingdom of Heaven, —it is for this reason that co-operating with the Lord's stewards at home, and following the example of the Lord Jesus, who Himself was a medical missionary, we desire to go forward, see the work extended, and His name glorified."

Some account of a journey taken by Miss Jay, from Tangier to Tetuan, in company with Mr. and Mrs. Mackintosh, of the Bible Society, will help to show the value of the medical work in opening doors even in distant places.

"*May* 16*th*, 1887.—We started from Tangier about 4 p.m., having only a ride of about two hours to our first camping place,—Mr. and Mrs. Mackintosh, their colporteur and I, with a soldier and four men in charge of the pack animals. We had a lovely ride among the hills till we reached Beni Wassine, the village where we were to spend the night. Several of the villagers gathered round to watch the erection of the tents, and soon recognised me as the Tabeeba (lady doctor) from the Marshan. We have had many patients from here, and I hope to see some old friends in the morning.

"In the morning Mrs. M. and I visited many of the huts, among them that of Haji Ali, a man whom we all like and trust, and who is acting as our guide on this journey. He has often asked me to come and stay a few days with his wife and daughters. We know him so well, I had almost promised to do so, but was not prepared to find it such a wretched dirty place, for he is quite a fine fellow. In all the huts we were saddened by the utter darkness and ignorance of the poor women. They seem to know nothing of higher things, and to have very little wish to know; but they all listen quietly to what is said. Some, however, were brighter, and seemed interested in the Scripture pictures which Mrs. M. showed and explained to them. It is a most lovely country, the ground a carpet of flowers, and large flocks of sheep and goats on the hills around, everything bathed in light and sunshine. Oh for the time when the true light shall shine in the hearts of the people!

"In the cool of the day I got a number of boys together, and Isa, the colporteur, taught them texts. To every one who learnt one I promised an Arabic text-card, and several of them gained the prize. All the evening afterwards the duller boys who had not been able to learn in class kept coming to repeat theirs, which the others had been teaching them, and get a card.

"18*th*.—Lovely day; all up early, packing and moving forward on the Tetuan road. I am riding a pack-horse, and get a fine view of the country. We cannot go quickly, because of the packs. About four we reached the Fundek, Waddiars, and encamped there. Mr. Macintosh and Isa were soon busy speaking to the men passing on the road, and also in the Fundek, which is very full. The animals all sleep in the centre, travellers and their goods in little open rooms all round. The whole is most disgustingly dirty; we were very thankful we were able to sleep outside.

"19*th*.—We are to remain here to-day, as there is a village near which Mr. and Mrs. M. wish to visit. I am not going with them, as my vaccinated arm is very painful. Had a quiet time resting and reading and speaking to some who passed: first, to two Jews—one could read well—then to a poor old woman walking alone all the way from Tangier to Tetuan. She would not come near, but stood a long way off, and whenever I mentioned the name of God, kissed her hand and bowed almost to the ground. Several times I had chats with boys, and gave text-cards to those who could read, but they need to be regularly instructed. Their ignorance strikes me more

MOORISH MOUNTAINEERS.

and more. Not only have they never heard the name of Jesus, but they do not seem to know they have souls, nor to be interested, except in what concerns the present everyday life. Late in the afternoon a group of youths arrived from the village, saying that Mr. and Mrs. M. were returning, and they had come for medicine for a sick woman. I had a nice talk with them. They were much interested in my pencil, notebook, and other little things, asking me again and again to write before them. Afterwards Mrs. M. and I went into the Fundek to talk to the poor women. They were very tired with their journey, almost too tired to talk or listen.

"21st.—We had a long ride yesterday; were all up at five taking down the tents, and starting off again on the Tetuan road. After some distance we branched off across the hills to reach a village which has not been often visited. It was a long, hot, but very lovely ride; the mountainous scenery grows finer the further we go. The people seem proud of their beautiful country, and pleased when they see how much we admire it. We encamped on the most breezy spot we could find, close to the village of Midhan. After dining and resting I sat for some time listening to Mrs. M. reading and speaking to a number of men who had come to see what we wanted. We then went to visit the villagers. In every place we find the same ignorance and darkness and dirt; but as yet we have also always found a kind welcome, all the hospitality they have it in their power to offer, and quiet attention to what we have to say. At first they are shy, having rarely seen foreigners, and sometimes their curiosity overcomes their politeness, and they overwhelm us with amusing questions just when we hope they are interested in higher things. We could not stay long, but they begged us to return, so this morning I set off early for the village, and had a happy time there, for quite a nice group of women collected as soon as I arrived. They kindly drove off the dogs for me. At every village there are a number of hungry, savage-looking creatures, and it is hardly safe to enter till some of the people send them off. The women took me into a large hut. As usual it was without windows, and almost pitch dark, the little low door being crowded up by women. I could hardly see anything at first, but as my eyes grew accustomed to the place I discovered that, besides the women and children, there were two cows, three dogs, and several chickens in the hut. I sat down rather unwillingly, the place was so indescribably dirty, but they would not let me stand. As usual, they commenced asking me questions, feeling my clothes, taking off my gloves, etc. At last we got to higher things. I found one boy could read well, and gave him a text-card. This started a conversation, and I tried to explain the Gospel to them with the help of the Wordless Book. One woman strongly objected to being told that her heart was black. 'No,' she said, 'it is clean; not quite clean like that page; there is a little black, for I have done some wrong things, but not much.' Before leaving I sang them some hymns, the children joining in one of the choruses. They seemed to enjoy singing it over several times. Returning, went to read and rest under the olive trees. There are several truly lovely groups of them about here, and their shade is most refreshing. The people in these poor villages have very little money, and the colporteur has been exchanging books for milk, vegetables, eggs, and even snuff.

"In the afternoon we all rode across the river to a village called Mikam. We found the people really afraid of us; they all ran away at first, and even afterwards, when they allowed us to come and talk with them, they none of them wanted us in their houses. Mr. M. found the men bigoted and unwilling to be spoken to. Before we left they grew a little more friendly. These places need to be visited often that they may learn to trust us and feel we are their friends, otherwise they do not listen to our message. In Tangier and the neighbourhood, or in any place from which we have had patients, we never have this difficulty; they know we wish to help them and do them good.

"*Sunday.*—Such a happy day. We feel we have so much for which to thank the dear Lord, for all has gone well since we started. He has filled our hands with work, for everywhere we find open doors, and we are all keeping well; indeed, already we all feel much better and stronger for being so much in the fresh, beautiful air.

"Mr. M. had a service in Arabic at ten a.m.—all the servants and several men from the village. It was nice to watch their faces: they really listened eagerly. Even though they do not approve of what is said, many of the men seem to enjoy hearing Arabic well read and spoken. They did not weary at all, though the service lasted an hour and a half. Afterwards we went and sat under the olives, Mr. and Mrs. M. speaking to quite a large number of men and boys there.

"In the afternoon we visited the further part of the village, where we had not been before. When we turned home, we left Mr. M. and the colporteur still talking to a large group of men outside the village. In the day several came for books. We pray and believe some of this precious seed will fall into good ground. The people wish us to stay and live amongst them.

"*25th.*—Ramadan began, which we fear we shall find a hindrance to our work in every way. We started early, and rode over the hills to visit the little village of Ansak; we were much disappointed to find it almost deserted, all the people being out in the fields harvesting. It is the most beautiful spot we have yet seen, a little paradise of trees, rocks, waterfalls, gorgeous flowers, and lovely maidenhair and other ferns; the little huts dotted about amongst them in the most picturesque fashion, and all on the side of a steep hill commanding glorious views. They tell us the people here are always well; however, we found one man very ill with fever, with whom and his wife we had some conversation. We promised him medicine if he could send for it to Tetuan. He seemed almost too ill to take any interest in what we said to him about Christ. A few men went to speak with Mr. M. outside the village.

"Notwithstanding the wind, we found our tents almost unbearably hot on our return. I went to see a poor widow with a number of children, in whom we had been interested yesterday. I had promised to return to-day, and they were expecting me. The poor children had each

FOREST OF OLIVES.

gathered me a bunch of flowers, and were distressed at my coming so late, as the flowers had faded. Quite a group of women and children gathered round. I tried to speak to them of Christ, but found it hard to get their attention, they wanted to ask so many questions about my country, etc.

"28th.—To-day we visited a large Sok among the hills, the first I have ever been to, and I shall never forget the impression it made on me. Riding there, the heat was intense, but the country so lovely it made one forget it. A great part of the way we rode by the side of a river, the banks thick with oleander and wild roses, the ground covered with cistus, everlastings, and a hundred other flowers.

"Sok el Khamis is held on the top of a small hill, and to it, from all the villages far and near, come the people bringing animals and goods for sale. It is a grand holiday for them all; they are all in their best clothes, and it is evidently the event of the week to them. They erect little booths, with boughs of trees, and under them spread out their goods for sale. The women mostly sit under the trees, and sell chickens, eggs, and all kinds of native garments. They sling their babies in towels to the trees, giving them a shake now and then to keep them rocking.

"It was interesting to watch the long lines of people winding down from the mountain villages. Mr. M. said it reminded him of the great communion meetings in country places in Scotland. How it made us long for the time when the people of this land shall come trooping in from all parts to hear of Christ, and celebrate His love to them.

"While we were resting before going to the Sok, an old man, a former patient, found me out, and gave me a warm welcome. He seemed surprised to find me so far from Tangier, said he was quite well, and thanked me many times for what we had done for him. It was such a pleasure so soon to find a friend among these thousands of people. He gave proof of his gratitude in a very acceptable way. We were all dreadfully hot and thirsty, and had sent into the Sok for some oranges, but there was not one to be had. He must have seen we were disappointed, for after a time he returned and gave us five. He must have got them from friends, for there were none for sale. When Mrs. M. and I went into the Sok to buy a few things, a great crowd gathered round us. We had two of our men with us. We did not dare stop long in one place, it seemed as if the whole market collected about us. They were all perfectly kind and polite, only so intensely interested in the English ladies. Finding we could understand them, they poured out a torrent of Arabic, and kept calling to me to take off my veil. The crowd was so large, we could hardly breathe, and had to tell the men at last to make a way for us to escape. Seeing these crowds of people all in darkness, hardly any of them knowing the name of Christ, made us long for the voice of an angel to shout to them, above all the din and confusion, the glad tidings of a Saviour's love. There was so little one could do in the midst of that surging crowd, only tell them that we belonged to the Lord Jesus, that we loved them and their country, and had left ours because we wanted to speak to them about the Messiah whom we knew and loved. Later on, the Lord gave us an opportunity of speaking of Him; for while we were resting, to my delight another old patient came up, a woman of some influence. She nearly smothered me with caresses, said she had heard I was coming to the Sok, and brought a sick child for me to see—would we come to her under the trees a little way off? We went, and found a large crowd of women seated, and they made a place for us in the centre. Directly the people found we were there, they all began again to collect round us. Again it seemed as if all the market were flocking to us, the women first, and the men in a great ring outside, but we did not mind, the circle of women sitting prevented our being crowded, and secured us enough air. There we stayed a long time, speaking of Christ and the forgiveness of sins which He alone can give, to all whom our voices could reach. They listened, and were quieter than we expected. My friend had introduced me as the Tabeeba of Sidna Aisa, and said we both loved God very much. It all was so new to them, yet they listened earnestly, often saying, 'Good, good!' These people are so kind, so loving; they grow dearer to me every day, and it was a real delight to me to be thus surrounded by them. I saw the sick child. She is very ill, and I told the woman to take her to the doctor as quickly as possible.

"In the afternoon we all rode to the village of Kallallu, a long lovely ride up the steep mountain opposite, through narrow lanes, so thick sometimes with creepers we could hardly push through. The village was very scattered, and most of the people were away in the fields; but Mrs. M. and I found a most interesting family living in quite a good house—they were taking charge of it for a rich Moor.

"They were a large merry party, several girls and children, three married daughters, and the mother. They gave us a warm welcome, were delighted to have such unusual visitors, and much interested in everything about us. Though very talkative, they grew quiet when Mrs. M. spoke to them of Christ, and two of the elder women seemed really interested, asking several questions. It was difficult at first to make them understand what sin is. They were most unwilling to let us go, and begged us to bring the tents and come and stay beside them. They brought us eggs and apricots, and gave us more than we liked to take."

The journal goes on to tell of some most interesting visits paid to wealthy families in Tetuan, but the details may not be published.

"*June* 1st.—Had a most interesting morning in the town. On our return to the tents, found three out of the four had been blown down, and it soon began to pour with rain. Everything got soaked, and we were obliged hastily to move into a little house which fortunately had been found in the town. We are so thankful to have this place of shelter, but sorry, on account of the storm, to be obliged to give up going again to the great market tomorrow—we had intended starting for it this afternoon.

"We all rode across the river this afternoon to the village of Kittom, on the mountain opposite. The road was very bad, like a narrow water-course, with much mud; but on arrival we had a most friendly reception. The miller bought a Testament, and a very large number of men gathered round Mr. M. The women carried off Mrs. M. and me in different directions to see their gardens and houses. They have oranges, figs, and pomegranates in abundance, and lots of lovely flowers. They begged us to stay and live with them, and some seemed really interested in the 'Old, old story,' which was so new to them. They gave us milk to drink, and filled my basket with eggs. They were so affectionate we felt very sorry to have to leave them so soon. They told us of a village far away, almost on the peak of the mountain, where no strangers can go, and made us laugh by telling us that the women there when they let their children out to play, tether them by a cord to the trees lest they should fall over the side of the mountain. We hope to reach them another time."

These fragmentary extracts from journals can convey but a very slight idea of the steady work which is carried on day by day, both in Tangier itself, and branching out from it in various directions; but it is work which we know must tell, for it is sowing the seed of the Word, that incorruptible seed, which God has promised to use in the conversion and salvation of souls.

In Tangier, within the last year, a work has begun among the Spaniards settled there, which has been a great joy to the missionaries. Quite a number, about twenty, have openly confessed Christ in baptism. The little room in which they used to meet in the town became so much too small that a larger meeting-place had to be sought; and what used to be a very low theatre has been rented, and changed into a place where God is worshipped, instead of dishonoured. One of the missionaries, Mr. Patrick, has devoted himself to this branch of the work.

Three young men, Messrs. Summers, Mensink, and Edwards, have been trying to win their way in Tetuan, but their difficulties, so far, have been great. The customs of the country prevent men from getting access to Moorish houses, and the people do not accord to them the same welcome that they give to ladies.

Mr. Summers lately made a journey into the mountains, to a town called Sheshewan, but his life was in very great danger, the people being opposed to any Christian intruding into what, for some reason, they consider a holy place. Mr. Summers was kept virtually a prisoner in one of the filthy cells of the fundak, both in size and odour something worse than an English pigsty. The Kaid forbade his going out into the town at all, and from the temper of the people it is probable that his life would have been taken had he done so. Unwilling to leave without telling his message, and hoping for a more favourable turn of affairs, Mr. Summers stayed on for a week. He was visited by numbers of men, who came to denounce him and threaten to kill him if he did not acknowledge Mohammed as the prophet of God; and to all who came, as far as they gave him opportunity, he preached the Gospel. Even in that fanatical crowd two who came heard the word with interest, and gladly received copies of the New Testament. At the end of a week it seemed plain that nothing more could be done, and Mr. Summers, with the Kaid's consent, set out on his return journey. The women in the villages he passed through screamed and called upon the men to shoot the Nazarene who was defiling their country, and it was not till he had forded a river and got well out of this inhospitable region that he could breathe freely, and give vent to his feelings in thanksgiving to Him who had kept him hidden under the shadow of His wings. These poor people do not yet know their true friends; but we cannot doubt that prayer and patient work will open a way for the Gospel even there.

CHAPTER VIII.

Fez.

WILLIAM CAREY'S MOTTO:
*Expect great things from God.
Attempt great things for God.*

THE short visit paid to Fez in the spring of 1888 only increased Miss Herdman's desire to make it a centre for Mission work, and at the close of a few months spent in England to recruit her health, she went back, determined, if possible, to remain there. The country was at that time in a very disturbed state; the Sultan was at the head of his army engaged in putting down attempts at insurrection among various Hill tribes, and friends in England feared that the usual dangers of travelling would be multiplied. Miss Herdman promised to consult the British representative in Morocco, Sir Kirby Green, before taking any step, but as his opinion was that she could go with safety where others could not, the journey was at once arranged for. Accompanied by Miss Copping, a trained nurse from Westminster Hospital, and Miss Reed, who had but lately arrived, and was only beginning to learn Arabic, she set out once more on the trying and tedious journey in October, 1888. It was accomplished without difficulty, the weather being fine, but as they did not take the most direct route it occupied ten days. As usual, they were obliged to have and to pay for a soldier as a guard, though his guardianship could have been merely nominal, as the one appointed for them was so old and infirm that he could not get off or on his mule without assistance. Arrived at Fez, their first necessity was to find a house, and this by God's goodness, through the help of kind friends, was soon arranged. Like all Moorish houses the rooms are without windows, light and air being admitted not very freely by the doors which open into a small court. The court itself is roofed over, but has a large aperture at the top closed only with iron bars across it. Besides the rooms on the ground floor, which are used for receiving patients, there are two upper ones opening on a balcony, and a small chamber on the flat roof. All the floors are of pretty bright-coloured tiles, and after walls and ceilings had been scrubbed and whitewashed, and packing cases transformed by womanly ingenuity into something like furniture, our friends addressed themselves to the work for which they had come. Two days a week were appointed for men and boys to come for medical treatment, and two other days for women.

A few extracts from Miss Herdman's most interesting journals must suffice to give an idea of the work.

"On Thursday, besides those who came for medicine, we had a party of young Shereefs in, who asked a great many questions about our religion. They only came to pass the time, but we have Thursday as one of the men's days, because it is a school holiday, and the teachers and scholars, who are the good readers, can come in. These young men sat a long time listening to the Scriptures read and hymns sung, and they say they will come again. The men and boys having minds trained to a certain degree by business or reading, are no trouble to us, and never interrupt us rudely, although we sometimes have animated discussions with them. Our point with them is that they are under a delusion in waiting until after death to be cleansed from sin, and that our Lord Jesus Christ is a present Saviour.

"Quite a number of people have heard the Gospel since our arrival. Some are reading in their own houses Bibles and portions of Scripture lent to them.

"The harmonium is already a great attraction. Not only do the patients hear the hymns, but the little boys of the neighbourhood beg to come in to hear them. The men like the Eastern Arabic hymns out of the Beyrout hymn-book, and will often look over the book and try to join, but the women do not understand them, and we sing them easy doggerel in their own dialect. Those men who read understand the Syrian Arabic as it is like the Koran, but the poor and ignorant like the easy hymns the same as the women.

"Among the patients to-day was an old man who evidently expected a pair of new young eyes. He brought a saucepan for his eye-wash, and a basket of walnuts to the Tabeeba. Another patient brought a handsome piece of his own embroidery as a thank-offering, because he could now hear his watch tick, having been very deaf when he first came. Most of the people seem to be grateful, especially when their sick children are relieved. A good many female slaves come for medicine.

"Yesterday, among others, a woman came in bringing a little black slave, ten years old, diseased from head to foot. She said her sister had bought her fourteen months ago for £22, and she was then pretty and well, but two months after she was seized with this complaint. She evidently feared that she had made a bad bargain. I asked the child her story, and when encouraged to answer me by the woman who brought her, she said, 'I am from the Sous. I was stolen with a number of little girls from my village last year, and brought to Mogador, then here.' 'Did you ride or walk?' 'We rode on mules, several in each shwaree (panier) and one on the top. I was in a panier with another girl, five on the mule, but some mules carried more.' I remembered hearing last summer, how, after the Sultan had reduced the rebellious Sous to subjection, numbers of children were carried off, and that some were sold in Morocco city, but numbers had died on the journey, but when the Sultan heard of it, he put a stop to this disgraceful conduct on the part of his followers.

"The great Moorish festival of the birth of Mohammed terminated yesterday, its seventh day. We kept to the house while it lasted, as the streets were occupied from time to time by the Aissawa—wild, yelling fanatics, who are said to catch any unlucky Jews or Christians met with on their way, to toss them up in the air, and tear them to pieces on the way down —anyway, Jews and Christians avoid their path. We watched them from our apology for a window, singing and dancing with long dishevelled hair. Only separated from us by one house is the largest mosque in all North Africa, called 'The Cherubim.' We live on the

GALLERY OF MOORISH HOUSE.

borders of another great sanctuary. When we go out on foot, which is but seldom, we meet crowds of worshippers from both, and as some are very fanatical, we hurry through the streets.

"*January 3rd*, 1889.—A lovely bright day. Praise the Lord, the climate here agrees with us, and we are in good health and spirits. There has been very heavy, seasonable rain; the higher Atlas mountains are deep in snow, the nearer spurs, of which we have a view from our roof, get covered with snow in showery weather, but a sunny day or two melts it. To-day we had about fifty men and boys, principally patients. One came both morning and afternoon to read the Bible with us. Several returned portions of Scriptures, and had others to take away. Five of the patients were from a party of Berbers, who came lately from Morocco city to bring a present to the Sultan. They spoke the Shluh language, but two of their number also understood Arabic well. One had a gunshot wound, and also asked for medicine for one of their saints with a similar wound. Our man had no patience with them, seeing they begged for medicine not only for themselves, but for their friends in Morocco. 'They are all highway robbers and murderers,' he said. But remembering that Jesus Christ came into the world to save sinners, Miss Copping sent them away with all their numerous wants supplied, and I tried to impress upon them the need of true repentance and of a Saviour. To-day a good many female slaves were treated, some old friends, some new cases. One young woman, who has often come, said to me to-day, 'I do so like coming here. I had a feverish attack and was prevented from coming last week, and missed you all. My master has been in Egypt and likes Christians, and he said to me to-day, "Go and hear about Jesus Christ."' 'Then you have a kind master.' 'Yes, but some are very cruel; Mohammedans say it is no sin to beat or strangle a black.' Three of the Sultan's slaves came to-day, of the families of his muleteers. These poor women belong to the outer courts of the Palace; they listened very intelligently to the Gospel.

"We have had a very busy day; seventy-eight women have been treated. We have endeavoured to teach each group, but sometimes the number of women talking together has been rather overpowering. The harmonium is in great request. A poor slave girl, who had to wait a long time for her turn, came in from the court again and again and joined her sweet voice in the easy hymns. She said she had been asking every day since the last time she had come for medicine, for a clean heart. Some of the women are beginning to sigh over their sins, especially the one that most easily besets them—hatred. When I asked one woman the cause of the illness from which she had recovered through treatment here, she said, 'I am one of four wives; I do not know what the others may have given me.' They are very cruel in this country, and often give a person enough poison to injure them for life without absolutely killing them.

"Among those who came to-day was a man who turned out to be the nephew of a Kaid who had showed us kindness last summer while we were encamped at a large village. This man told us he had heard the Gospel from one of the muleteers from his neighbourhood, who had brought us to Fez the first time, and had last month in his company been to the Arabic meeting at Hope House. He told me he loved the Lord Jesus Christ, and asked for a Bible. He spent the day with us, and on leaving gave my hand a warm shake, and said, 'I hope to come and see you again; I love the Lord Jesus like you.' Gladly I gave him a small Bible. Miss Caley and I had earnestly prayed many times for that village; here is the answer.

"We have news from Tangier that S. H., who heard of Christ from us in Larache and took care of us in Fez in the summer, has confessed Christ in

A MOHAMMEDAN AT PRAYER.

baptism. Yesterday was an especially interesting men's day. Among those who came for medicine were a good many who were seriously disposed and inclined to read the Gospel. But best of all were two men from Tarradunt, a town in South Morocco, who came in and asked for the New Testament. One said that Jesus was the only Saviour, and that He died and rose again; the other looked very bright, and assented to all I said without speaking. They both went out suddenly, and I had no opportunity of seeing them alone, or inviting them to come on Sunday, but we hope they may turn up on Monday, as they know the house is open to men on that day. I think they must have learned from some of the scattered persecuted Christians of Mogador.

"To-day I had an hour's conversation, mostly on spiritual things, with a Moor who has shown us real disinterested kindness. He embraces such opportunities of hearing, but is, like many others afraid to show his interest in the Gospel before his very fanatical fellow-citizens. He said, 'If my best friends heard me say what I have said to you now, they would kill me.' How real the exhortation of Christ, 'Fear not them that kill the body.' No one wants to kill us in England, and we read such passages and think nothing of them. Here we pray to be delivered from the fear of man, and the Lord has granted the desire of our hearts.

"The Spring rains have set in, and the streets of Fez are rivers of black, fœtid mud. Outside the town the grain is very thick, and is coming on rapidly.

"We go out clothed in a white woollen burnoos, the hood fastened round the head with a white silk cord. Mouth and nose are covered with one piece of white muslin and the forehead with another, both tied round the head under the burnoos, the eyes alone are visible. I am known by my spectacles, otherwise the disguise is perfect. The people of Fez not having mixed with Europeans, do not think any woman unveiled respectable. They will learn in time. The want of roads between Fez and the coast has isolated them, so that they have scarcely changed in the thousand years since the city was founded, while the rest of the world has advanced in education and civilization.

"We observe that the women are much more attentive to the Gospel than they were formerly. A slave, who was here to-day, with her child, who is under treatment, understands the Gospel very well, and loves to hear of Jesus. I take especial pleasure in teaching the slaves. Many of them have forgotten their parents in the Sahara and the Soudan, and listen with great pleasure to hymns and words about a Father in Heaven and a Saviour who cares for them. Others are fanatical, and say they have God and the prophet and want nothing more.

"The men's days are very interesting. We had some good scholars in to-day, who read the Gospel with me; also some from wild tribes near Fez. These were Arabs; often we have Riffs and Shluhs, each with their own language, but making themselves understood in Arabic. All these wild tribes rob and murder as opportunity offers. It seemed to be quite a new idea to one of the men to-day to hear that if he killed travellers, or stole, and did not repent, he would go to hell.

"I try to teach these country people especially that as they expect their children to please them, and are glad when they help them, so God loves them, and wishes them to do His will. Although utterly uneducated, except in vice, they understand similes very well, and one understands why our Lord taught in parables. Four times a week, besides the townspeople, who tell lies, hate one another, and are covetous and cruel, we have people to teach who habitually steal and murder. It is a great privilege to be the first to speak to them of repentance unto life, and of a Saviour from Satan, whom they recognise as the tempter who overcomes them. Now that the roads are drying and the snow melting, men and women come two and three days' journey for medicines from parts never visited by Europeans, and where few native travellers pass, and they at the risk of their lives. The poorest man, if clothed in a coarse white jelab not in rags, is likely to be murdered for the sake of it. People are often murdered almost under the shadow of the walls of Fez, for all the tribes around are wild.

MOORISH GIRL.

"We have had several persons from a small town called Sifroo, about twelve miles distant, and we propose visiting it, if the Lord open the way. We have invitations from families whose members are sick, and we desire to take the Gospel of the grace of God to a city still in total darkness. There are a good many Jews there, but the main population is Mohammedan."

The visit to Sifroo was carried out during the hottest weeks of summer, when Miss Herdman and her companions were glad to escape from the stifling atmosphere of the city. They found a lodging at Sifroo after some difficulty, in a native hotel. The heat of the sun was great, but the abundant shade of the irrigated gardens and orchards round the town was pleasant, and there they spent much of their time, reading and conversing with the owners.

The following account of the visit to Sifroo is from Miss Copping:—

"We spent nearly two months in this little town on the side of a mountain, exploring the neighbourhood, making friends with the people, doctoring the sick, and preaching the Gospel to rich and poor.

"As we went there from Fez the whole country seemed one mass of luxuriant green, mingled with brilliant flowers of every hue, and as we neared Sifroo, although tired and hot with our long ride and the midday sun, we could not help admiring the exquisitely-tinted fruit blossoms and the sparkling streams flowing through the gardens. On our return journey, two months later, what a change had come over everything! The green hills were brown and bare, the valley and plains a dusty, stony waste, the poor sheep and goats trying in vain to find grass sufficient for their need.

"We found almost as many Jews as Moors in Sifroo, but we were welcomed by all, rich and poor alike. The Moslems there are not as religious, and therefore not as bigoted as those of Fez. We visited numbers of the houses. At one house to which Miss Reed and I went, the lady took us in with great delight to see some wonders from our own country. We found her walls plastered over with advertisements of candles, chocolate, etc. The house was beautifully clean, and the lady let in a few of her neighbours, who listened attentively to what we told them of the Saviour; but she herself was so fussy, asking again and again what she should give us to eat, fanning away flies and sweeping up some fancied dust, while the neighbours, especially one young woman, were anxious to hear our message. It was truly wonderful the kindness we strangers received from these people.

"A poor little orphan boy, sadly diseased, who had been under our care many months in Fez, called upon us in Sifroo soon after the great feast. I enquired how he had fared during the holiday. He said, 'It was this way, Tabeeba, I was there ; and if they asked me to eat I did, and said, "May the Lord bless and reward you;" and if they did not ask me to eat I did not, and said, "May the Lord have mercy on your soul."' He stayed with us several days, but we had to present him with everything he used or touched, as he is a leper. We are very sorry for him.

"One acquaintance we made was a bright, kind young man from Tedla. He belongs to a very warlike tribe, and even he, loving as he is, has a little of the savage left in him. He came to teach us Shluh, and did his very best to teach us the most useful words in a short time. He is much loved by the Sifroo children, as well as by the grown people. He tries all he can to help the people from the mountains when they come in to market, and they often need a helper from the oppressions of the Kaid. He was very much taken by what he heard of our Lord, and would listen intelligently, asking many questions. He said he knew that Si Moses belonged to the Jews, and Si Aisa to the Christians, but who did Si David belong to? He thanked God when he heard that Moses and David, as well as our Lord Jesus belonged to the sons of Adam, to him as well as to us, that God so loved the world that He sent Jesus Christ into the world to seek and to save the sons of Adam. He seems almost a Christian, and we pray for him every day. He is so fearless that he would be a bright light.

"A baby boy was brought to me by his mother from a mountain tribe; the little one was suffering from ophthalmia. When he saw me he exclaimed, 'Ya roumee' (O stranger), 'go to your own country at once.' When he saw that I did not obey him, he raised his tiny hand to strike me. This is the way the children are trained. He is the son of a chief, and feels it his duty to keep strangers from his country. A large party of women came from the same tribe, with their faces bleeding and sore as if they had been fighting with wild beasts. They told me that 'there had died to them a man.' I asked if he was husband, brother, or son to any one of them? They said he was not, but he was one of their tribe, and they had cried for fourteen days and torn their own faces, and they must not wash or change their clothes for three months. No wonder they were sick and feverish. There is so much that is intensely sad in this beautiful country.

"We were many times invited to a town named Ballin, where the people live in caves instead of houses, but we could not go without permission from the Kaid. After our return to Fez a chief called upon us with the desired permission. He said if we would go he would take great care of us and bring us back safely. We must share his cave; he would give us all we wished for, and protect us from robbers. The robbers are a very real evil. The young man who taught us Shluh often warned us, 'It is not your goods they will steal; it is you.'

"It would take too long to tell of all our pleasant rides, walks, visits, medical mission days, etc. We treated more than 130 patients every week, many of them from the mountains round, so that God's Word has gone far and wide. May the Lord Himself water it with His Holy Spirit."

The next extract is from Miss Herdman, written while still at Sifroo:—

"Everything about this place is novel and interesting. Having to do with three races essentially different one from the other, Arabs, Berbers, and Jews, makes our work and our recreation alike varied.

"The town is surrounded by gardens, extending (roughly speaking) a mile in every direction; the outer fringe of all is like a park, planted with very large and fruitful olive trees. We walked out to one extremity of the plantations this morning, and then returned and sat in a garden. As we sit in their gardens we open a portion of God's Word and read to the learned, and speak and sing to the ignorant.

"Every inch of ground is irrigated; the water is turned on and off at stated times to each of the gardens. The mountain stream we skirted this morning, with its sparkling water and cascades, its fringe of maidenhair ferns and tangle of blackberries and honeysuckle, was indescribably refreshing. Sifroo is a natural paradise, and its poor but industrious inhabitants make the best of its resources. Spiritually it is dark indeed, but we are privileged day by day to be its light-bearers. Jews and Moors look over our Bibles and Testaments, and we feel sure that our few weeks' holiday here has not been lost time. We visit the homes of rich and poor, we climb the mountains and frighten the authorities, who fear a murderous attack upon us. The other day when they could not frighten us with Berbers they spoke of snakes. We have heard since that one very interesting mountain we have climbed twice has very large dangerous snakes hid in its caves, which are large and inviting, and in one of which we proposed spending the day.

"We have at present as a guest a Berber woman from the mountains, from a village with only one path to it up the rock. The inhabitants turn on a mountain stream at will, and laugh at an enemy below. She has taken refuge with us from the oppression of a Kaid, who had taken her mule. We have been trying to get justice for her for two days, and to-morrow we are promised success, and we hope to send her and it home safely.

"We had Moors reading the Bible with us until dusk to-day, and then spoke to Jews and Moors in the Fundak court. A Fundak such as we are lodging in is a place with great opportunities of making known the Gospel. The Moorish Passover feast has just ended, work has begun again, and the Fundak is full of travellers to-night, with their beasts of burden. A large quantity of wool and of cedar beams have arrived from the mountains, and will go to Fez early to-morrow morning.

"Among other readers to-day we had one who has not been here before, and who is in a Government post, in which taking bribes is usual. We read the 15th Psalm, and New Testament passages. He was much impressed, and we spoke together of the possibility of being honest, and yet not miserably poor. 'Without lies one cannot live,' is a common saying here. How often I think of David preaching *righteousness* in the great congregation. He heard with much pleasure about a Saviour from sin."

At the beginning of September a little rain fell, which made the earthen floors of the Fundak damp, and caused the bad smells to rise, so Miss Herdman and her companion had to return to Fez, though the heat there was still great.

There we leave these three brave women, alone in the midst of an alien people, yet not alone, for He who said "Lo am I with you alway, even to the end of the world," is with them. The love of Christ constraineth them, and it is by the power of that Divine love breathed into their souls, and shining in their lives, that they, and all the rest of the noble band of true missionaries throughout the world, must win and conquer. There are many different opinions about the best ways of carrying on missionary work, but one thing seems clear, that sooner or later there will be success wherever love abounds—love which suffereth long and is kind, love which vaunteth not itself and is not puffed up; love which beareth all things, believeth all things, hopeth all things, endureth all things; love which never faileth. Such love, which can take to its heart the loathsome and the sinful, is indeed, a part of the Divine nature of which God's children are called to be partakers. Many waters cannot quench it, neither can the floods drown it, and wherever it is fully in exercise, it must prevail.

CHAPTER IX.

Tunis.

Toi dont l'âme est tourmentée
Aux approches de la mort,
Toi dont la nef ballotée
Ne sait où trouver le port,
Regarde, à travers tes larmes
Ce phare qui, tant de fois
A brillé dans mes alarmes,
C'est la croix, c'est la croix!

HE country of Tunis is that corner of the North African coast where the Mediterranean makes a sudden bend southwards, just opposite Sicily, and washes a coast-line of about 350 miles facing east, before it again resumes its usual direction. The town of the same name is situated at the head of a bay before the angle is reached, therefore facing northwards. What was once a splendid harbour, communicating with a land-locked lagoon, is now so silted up that ordinary steamers cannot approach nearer to the town than about four miles, which makes landing there inconvenient.

With an area of about 60,000 square miles, and a coast-line of 550 miles, the country does not contain more than two millions of inhabitants, the small population being probably attributable to Turkish misrule. Until the sixteenth century Tunis was one of the independent Barbary States, but since that time it has been subject to Turkey, governed by a Bey, owing allegiance to the Sultan. In 1881, however, the French forcibly took it under their protection, so that everything now is very much under their influence. After assuming the Protectorate, a French army marched to Kairwan, a curious ancient city situated inland. Until the French invasion it had been as carefully secluded and guarded from the intrusion of

A STREET IN TUNIS.

any Christian as Mecca itself, and was considered nearly as sacred, being the place of burial of "My Lord the Companion," an intimate friend of Mohammed, who, during his lifetime, and afterwards in death, wore always on his breast a portion of the prophet's beard, in token of his devotion to him. For a thousand years, so far as can be ascertained, no Christian foot ever trod the streets of Kairwan, or Christian eye looked upon its sacred places. Before its surrender to the French, however, this strictness had somewhat relaxed. A few privileged English travellers were permitted by the Bey to enter, though, once within the walls, care was taken to let them see as little as possible. Now the splendid mosques are open to public gaze, and even the sacred spot where "My Lord the Companion" lies entombed in marble, surrounded with a gilded lattice, has been looked upon by the hated, feared, and despised Nazarene, a striking proof of the decay of Moslem power.

The range of Atlas Mountains which extends from Morocco eastwards, ends in Tunis. The Berbers of the mountain villages are still called Kabyles, as in Algeria; many of them are to be found in the town itself, where they work as gardeners and labourers. As in Algeria, the population is made up of a mixture of Moors, Arabs, Kabyles, Turks, and Jews, with many Europeans in the towns. The Moors descended from those who were driven from Spain in the time of Ferdinand and Isabella, form an almost separate and very aristocratic class by themselves. They are said to preserve carefully the rusty keys of their forefathers' houses in Andalusia, and to hand them down from father to son in the hope of one day regaining their possessions.

Into this mixture of races, all alike needing the blessed healing, enlightening, purifying influences of the Gospel of Jesus Christ, has gone a little band of workers, few and feeble, and utterly unable of themselves to cope with the forces of evil, yet having their hands made strong by the hands of the Mighty One.

Two French brethren, M. Bureau and M. Mercadier, with their wives, were the first to occupy the place. They have succeeded in opening a small book-shop, where also they receive any who are willing to converse and read the Scriptures with them. They have also held evening meetings in French, resembling Mr. McAll's "Conferences" in Paris.

Only a year ago the mission was reinforced by three English ladies, and though, of course, their Arabic is still very defective, it is wonderful how quickly doors are opened to them which are closed against men, and how soon they have been able to come into real heart-contact with the people. They have been guided to find a suitable house, a genuine Moorish one, and quite in the Arab part of the town. While busy in acquiring the language, they are at the same time making friends with many families, either through helping them in time of sickness, or being brought into contact with them in other ways. Already they have sufficient Arabic to be able to use these opportunities for reading the Scriptures and speaking of the Saviour they love. Some extracts from journals will best describe the work begun in Tunis, although not greatly differing from that carried on in other parts of North Africa. The first extracts are from a letter by Miss Grissell :—

"Now to tell you something of our Arab friends, and how we are trying to help them. We have as many homes open to us as we know how to visit—indeed, more than we can visit constantly. Miss Harding has been able to help so many with her knowledge of medicine that we are hailed at the doors as we pass, to go in and see the sick. I must tell you of the difficulties in helping the sick here, for they are not small, as the men even are like children over a glass of medicine, and *many* times we have been quite unable to persuade a man to take a second dose. There was a poor fellow almost dying from fever, and yet he would not touch quinine a second time.

"A fortnight ago we spent two days at the seaside house of a Moor, in whose family we have visited a great deal here. Their manner of life was very strange to us, and apparently we were equally strange to them, for they seemed always watching to see what we were going to do next. Their home is situated in a little village on a high rock, a picturesque little place, very Arabic. I wish I could paint the little market-place as we saw it from one of the windows, with the pretty fruit shop in front, and so alive with business in the early morning. Some of the women are here allowed a little more liberty, and are permitted to go down the rocks and find a quiet corner to bathe, but our friends were never allowed outside the door, nor even at the window to look out; and, happily, seem to have lost all desire from its very hopelessness. You may fancy how glad the three dear women were to see us, and how they assured us we were no trouble to them if we would only stay with them longer, but we could not then. At meal-times we had to manage without plates or knives, but we were given spoons and forks, and everybody put their spoon into whichever of the oily dishes they liked best. The old father and mother had their meals together; we dined with the two sons, and we could never persuade their wives to come and eat with us. It was very amusing to see one of the gentlemen piling his own fork with two or three nice bits, and then stretching over and placing them on the edge of a dish near us. At night we slept on the three divans in the sitting-room, and our manner of retiring to rest was such a cause of curiosity to all the women of the household, that they all assembled in the room to watch our proceedings.

"This visit was a grand opportunity for leaving the message behind us that our lips are so longing to deliver on all sides, and we each did our best with our different abilities.

"Miss Harding got the dear old father interested more than she ever had before. He seemed to enjoy having her sitting beside him with a Testament, and he with another, reading and asking her questions. It would indeed be grand if his heart were yielded to the Lord, for he has such power and influence in his family. The two sons came and read together with us each day once or twice, and the busy women we had to catch as best we could.

"There is another family in which we are much interested, and this, too, is one of good position and plenty of means. Their little invalid girl was the call into that house. Little Zabaida is an interesting child, aged eleven, who from a fall has severe curvature of the spine, and has lost all power in her legs. Miss Harding found her sitting up on her bed in a corner of a comfortable room, and there she had lived for eleven months, or more, bearing with the weakness and the suffering day by day as best she could, her mother and elder sister doing their best to soothe her, but their best was very little, for they had not even thought of carrying her out into the court for air. Miss Harding was able to obtain the loan of an electric battery for a month, and tried that constantly, but with almost no result. Her general health is somewhat improved. Some friend sent me out a very nicely dressed little doll, and I have often wished that she could have seen the pleasure it gave Zabaida. It is really a friend to her, always beside her.

"It is a large household of all ages, from an old negress, who is dying now, but was nurse to one of the parents, and is supposed to be close on a hundred years old, to the little boy of six years. Sometimes it is very difficult to get a quiet hearing; at present there seems so little real desire to hear the Gospel, the things of this life seem of so much greater interest. There is a young lad who reads Arabic well, and he is always a ready listener, and will try to silence the children and get a little quiet attention.

"I cannot tell you how painful it is to stand by a dying bed when the poor soul is passing into eternity, without having heard of the precious blood, of Jesus and of the gift of eternal life, and it is too late then, for the ear had lost its hearing. A page of the Koran was being monotonously read beside the dying negress, but what comfort could it convey even had she understood it! It made Miss Harding and me, as we stood there, wish we had come out sooner. Miss Harding spoke to those around of the solemnity of death, and its warning to all, but her words were only received with smiles. I do feel more and more out here how little is being done by Christians, who, having received such inestimable blessings themselves, are to a large extent leaving thousands to starve for the Bread of Life."

In the next extract, Miss Harding describes another visit a short way from Tunis:—

"Last Friday, I came to the little seaside village (Hammam el Enf), where the Mercadiers are staying. It is a primitive Arab village, about half an hour's distance by rail from Tunis. We live in three tiny cabins, in a long row of shanties, a little distance from the village, and close to the Mediterranean, only a narrow strip of sand and low parapet wall between us and it. Looking across the Bay of Tunis, in the distance Carthage can be dimly seen. We live out of doors, so have full benefit of sea-breezes, so invigorating after city life.

"Last evening I visited our landlord's wife, who is a Jewess; her sister and husband's partner came in as I was reading to her, and all listened so readily as I spoke to them of the Father's gift of His Son to be the Saviour of the world, and of the precious blood which alone can cleanse from all sin. As I read to them the words of the Lord to Nicodemus, 'Except a man be born again he cannot see the Kingdom of God,' they, like Nicodemus, marvelled, and as I went on to tell them how they could receive eternal life through Jesus, who is the Life, and that now they were in darkness, in death, the women said, 'This is all new to us, no one ever told us before.' As this cry, this time from Jewish women's lips, came home again to me, 'No one ever told me before,' I felt, 'Oh, that I *had* come sooner to tell you and others of the Saviour's love—you who have never heard of it.' It fired me with a deeper longing to seek to make known to the many thousands in Tunis and around, whose life is quickly passing away, and without having ever heard of Him, and for whom there is no hope beyond the grave. Oh, Christian sisters at home, who enjoy the privileges of Gospel light and liberty, who know the reality and joy of possessing the Lord Jesus as your life, and are seeking to follow Him closely, does not this cry which I pass on to you, as it now echoes in my own heart, awaken a response in yours? Here, as in India, are thousands of Mohammedan women (after twelve years of age, and earlier), prisoners in their own homes all their lifetime, to whom we alone can carry the message of life and peace. Until the husbands and brothers are brought to know Christ our lips alone can speak of Him to them; and how can we reach these thousands when every home must be visited separately, unless more labourers are sent forth? And for all these souls in each harem, each Arab court, Christ died—each soul is a blood-bought one. Think you it is nothing to Him that so many of these remain unsought, uncared for? Ah, no; His heart is yearning over each one, however degraded. If you could see as we daily see, the multitudes without any hope, who are living in such terrible darkness and sin, and feel the helplessness we feel in being able to reach so few amongst them, you would have the great need press on you, as it does on us. The time is so quickly passing; the night cometh when no man can work.

"Our first year in North Africa is just drawing to a close. Now we can testify to our Father's abiding faithfulness, and in the coming year would trust Him more fully yet. Jesus is enough for every need, and He becomes more and more real to each of us. May He make Himself known to the multitudes around us, to the glory of His name."

In addition to the work among Moors and Arabs, our friends have opened a room where addresses are given and hymns sung in French. They realise that the Gospel is to be preached to every creature, and that they, as

CAFE IN TUNIS.

bearers of the message, must leave out none to whom they have the opportunity of delivering it. The need for it among all classes and nationalities is plain. A Frenchman said to them that he had never come across a Christian; all who called themselves such that he had seen were people more to be avoided than sought. What need, then, that those who have the true light should let it shine out!

God has shown in Tunis that now, as of old, His Gospel is the power of God unto salvation to every one who believes. There have been some very encouraging cases, not only of reception of the Divine Word into the heart, but of open confession of the name of Christ; but as yet these cases are too new to be published. Only we would again beg Christians in England to whom the confession of their faith in the Lord Jesus is comparatively such an easy thing, not to forget those to whom it means so much more; involving certainly rejection by friends and nearest relatives, and loss of the means of livelihood, possibly imprisonment and torture.

As yet the work is confined to the town of Tunis. Other cities await the feet of God's messengers. On the coast there is Bizerta, with 5,000 inhabitants, Susa 8,000, and Sfaks 15,000. Inland lie other towns and villages, with the Kabyle villages scattered over the mountains, as in Algeria. Soon may the words of Isaiah, as repeated by Matthew, be fulfilled to them: "The people which sat in darkness saw great light, and to them which sat in the region and shadow of death, light is sprung up."

CHAPTER X.

TRIPOLI.

*Tidings sent to every creature,
   Millions yet have never heard;
Can they hear without a preacher?
   Lord Almighty, give the word.
Give the word; in every nation
   Let the Gospel trumpet sound,
Witnessing a world's salvation
   To the earth's remotest bound.*

N February, 1889, two young missionaries were sent to try what openings there might be in Tripoli. Mr. Michell, one of the two, had been in Tunis for about a year, chiefly occupied in learning Arabic. He is a born linguist, so it was hoped that he already knew enough of the language to serve for both, Mr. Harding having only just arrived from England. The latter has the advantage of some medical knowledge, although not a qualified practitioner, so the different gifts of the two have worked in well together. Considerable doubts were felt as to the possibility of carrying on any work for the Lord in a country still completely under Turkish rule, but there, as elsewhere, doors have been opened quite beyond our expectations, and the seed of the Word is being sown. That is all that man can do, but we look up in confidence to Him who alone can give the increase.

The coast of Tripoli is lower, and the country altogether less mountainous than further west, the Atlas Mountains shading off here into lower ranges of hills. The country around the town of Tripoli is thoroughly Oriental. Palm trees and cactus hedges, great wells, and fields with little canals for irrigation, combine, with droves of camels and picturesque but dirty Arabs, to remind the visitor that he is well to the East, and close to the Great Desert.

The missionaries began by visiting one or two of the purely Arab cafés for an hour in the evening, and while sipping their coffee, opportunities arose for conversation with those frequenting them. In this way, they soon made acquaintances which led on to further intercourse. Mr. Harding wished at first to keep his time free for study, but some inadvertent remark having led to the belief that he was a "tabib," or doctor, patients soon began to come to him.

"*March*, 1889.—We are looked upon as regular *habitués* of our café now, and the Lord has evidently made good our footing there. One gentleman had a good long read out of the New Testament to-night. The proprietor is a very bigoted Mohammedan, but of course so long as our sous are forthcoming he is not the man to make a fuss. Ahmed, a young man with whom we have made acquaintance, came in this evening to say he is going three days' journey into the interior with the Fezzan caravan. Mr. Michell gave him some Bibles, which he promised to give away. We asked if it would be possible for us to go. He said, Yes, but we should be killed before we got twenty miles from the city. He said, however, that if I would give the people medicine, I might go to Fezzan quite safely, they would take care of me.

"*May 1st.*—This month is the great fast of the Moslems, Ramadan; we find it out to our cost at night, for a man comes round twice in the night with a drum, with which he makes a most horrible noise. He has to wake up the faithful for their meals, and he takes good care to wake up everybody else too. The men are very quarrelsome this month, I suppose anybody would be who had nothing to eat from about 3 a.m. to 6 p.m. I saw a little boy to-night who had just been stabbed in the stomach by another boy. They say such things are very common during Ramadan. At the café to-night the proprietor told us his child had a fever of some sort, which had been going on for the last six weeks. He asked for some medicine for it, but I suggested that I had better see the child.

"This morning the café keeper came to take us to see his child. It was very ill, but I was glad to get a case which was not yet chronic or incurable, for hitherto they seem to have been hunting up all the ancient cripples of the city for me to cure.

"We gave the child some medicine, and to-night the café keeper said it was much better. He seemed very grateful to us, but I told him it was for the sake of the Lord Jesus, and then Mr. Michell told the story of the Good Samaritan, to which he listened very intently, and seemed to approve of it. He said he was sure that such doctrine was good, and went so far as to express his opinion that those who believe and act up to such teaching will not be condemned. He also quite appreciated the parables of the Lost Sheep and Lost Piece of Money. He utterly refused payment for our coffee. We went again to see the café keeper's child, and found her quite free from fever, and evidently on the high road to recovery. His wife was so delighted, that she came out herself to tell us how much better the child was, and he was so pleased he didn't seem to mind it.

"*June 1st.*—I was taken to see a girl who has been ill for the last six months. I suppose we may take it as a mark of confidence that we are brought into a house to see a Moslem woman. Her husband was very grateful. He wanted to give Mr. Michell 2 frs., but of course he would not take it. They seem to think there is something in the Christian religion, and told us they would pray for us.

" The husband of the young woman we are attending sent us a present of apricots, and he and his nephew came for medicine for themselves. We have given them a Gospel, which they say is very good.

" This morning, when I went to see the sick girl, they said she was worse; however, examination proved the contrary. All the urgent symptoms were gone, but she was evidently suffering for want of proper food and attention. I gave directions to her mother-in-law, and went home and made her a milk-pudding. Later in the day they sent to say she had eaten the pudding and liked it, and was much better, and would take as much of that kind of medicine as I liked to send her. One sees on every hand what need there is for work which ladies can do better than we can. More is to be done for most of these cases by proper nursing than by medicine, and while our medical work is only a means to an end, I feel sure there is a great opening for the attainment of that end by this means.

" Two days ago the husband of the girl I mentioned came to us in great trouble. He said she would not take her medicine, and wanted to go back to Arab treatment. He, poor fellow, was quite put out about it, for he was very grateful for what we had done, but he said she was very obstinate, and he thought he must let her have her own way. I had not seen her then for two days, so do not know how she was, but to-day I hear she is dead. From what I can gather, I expect they adopted some barbarous hot-iron treatment, which brought about collapse.

" This afternoon we went with one of our former patients to see his gardens out in the country. It was very pleasant, but it was very difficult to satisfy him in the way of eating fruit. We had to eat the whole time we were there, fill our pockets, and then he wanted to give us more.

" Thus ends another month, which has been one of progress, of getting deeper into the hearts of the people, getting more opportunities of proclaiming the Gospel and, above all, getting personally nearer to the Lord, getting more of His Spirit, without which all is worse than nothing. We feel that now Tripoli is certainly an established station, and that the work now begun in faith must be carried on till the Lord Himself shall come. May He grant to us, our helpers and successors, that measure of faith and love which we need in this great work for His glory."

The following extracts are from Mr. Michell's journal:—

"*March*, 1889.—We are getting better known. As we walk through the streets we are often saluted in the friendliest way by men we have met in cafés. Some even whom we do not recognise, especially negroes, wish us good-day with the broadest of smiles.

"*June 4th.*—Looking back over the last two or three months, I find that we have most distinct cause for great thankfulness to our Father in heaven, and much praise to His Name, for obstacles overcome, doors opened, and, on the whole, decided progress in the confidence of the people and their willingness to hear. From the bottom of our hearts we praise and thank Him, and give to Him all the glory for the marked improvement of our relations with the people, and the very encouraging prospects of the work.

"Last night, at the café we go to regularly, I had a long talk on the best of terms with a very pleasant old gentleman, who came to ask for some physic for his wife. He told me the Mohammedan belief about the Lord Jesus, and their account of the substitution of another Jew for Him at the crucifixion, and of their expectation of His return. 'But,' said he, 'when He does return He will declare Himself a true Moslem, and will expect His followers to repeat the formula, "There is no God but God, and Mohammed is the prophet of God!" and as for those that refuse——!' and he made a significant gesture with his stick.

"Well, one can only lay before them the truth—the Lord Jesus Christ as the only Saviour from sin and from death, the death of the soul, and righteousness in Him alone. It is of no use arguing about these beliefs of theirs. When the Holy Ghost has made them see their need of a Saviour, and convinced them of their lost condition, they will know that the one whom they need is the risen Son of God, and not a dead, helpless man, with a doubtful tale of his own inspiration, such as Mohammed.

"We have had occasion to go to the custom-house pretty frequently since coming here, and as it is always a long tedious business, we are well known to all the officials; indeed, with two or three we are quite on a familiar footing. I received a parcel the other day in which were several Arabic Gospels. They were examining these, and I took the opportunity to offer one to one of the chiefs. (They are all Turks, but many understand Arabic.) He took it, and asked me all about it, whereupon I explained the Gospel it contained. Others came and listened, and soon I had quite a crowd of Arabs, Turks, and Jews round his office, all listening with much apparent interest. The Effendi asked me to get him a Turkish Testament, which I promised to do. He came in and had dinner with us at the Arab restaurant we get our meals at yesterday.

"An Englishman who came to tea with us last week assured us that our lives are not safe without a revolver. He says that the many years he has been here and in the other towns of Tripoli convince him that the natives would gladly murder any 'unbeliever,' but they fear the Turks. But our God is a sure protection, and where traders and others go in fear of their lives after dark we are known as men of God, who sincerely seek their good. Such a thing as a man being asked into a Moslem's house for any reason whatever is, of course, unheard of, and yet the Lord takes His servants where He will, and that to bless both them and the natives. We hesitated at first to contract for a house for a whole year, but now we look

CAMEL AND DRIVER.

forward to a long and blessed time among these people. But we need the prayers of the Lord's people unceasingly, and with great faith, both for ourselves, that we may be kept very near to the Lord in this place where we have no spiritual fellowship with any of the Lord's servants, and also for our work among these fanatical people. For, after all, they certainly are fanatical, and our position here is, *humanly* speaking, rather precarious. And though I scarcely think we need fear religious persecution, yet outside the town robbers and highwaymen are numerous and dangerous.

"Last night we had one of the most remarkable experiences that perhaps ever fell to the lot of missionaries to Moslems. Till three o'clock in the morning we were preaching and discussing the Gospel with a whole society of 'howling dervishes.' We sat in the midst of them in their own meeting-house, telling the plan of salvation to their Sheikh, surrounded by his dervishes, after their exercises were over, and then most of them walked a part of the way home with us. But I will begin at the beginning, which is sad enough. In the afternoon a man came to the door and told me in English that he would like to have a talk with me. I asked him did he speak English, as he had a slightly foreign accent. 'I am an Englishman by birth,' he said, and when I asked him up into my room he said he had been converted to Mohammedanism nine years ago at Constantinople, and now he had dropped his English name, and was only known by a Turkish one. He said his object in coming was to speak to me about Islam, as he had heard that I was inquiring about it, and might be a likely convert. I said I should be delighted to have a talk with him; that was just what I was here for. He seemed sincere enough, and was all primed with the stock arguments of Mohammedanism. His great plea was works, holding that man was so weak and depraved that one good work that he did succeed in doing amply made up for the other lapses of his feeble human nature. I spoke to him long and seriously about his awful danger, trusting to good works without faith in Christ. I showed him that all our righteousness is but a soiled garment in the sight of God, and that by his deliberate rejection of the only Mediator he put himself outside of all hope of eternal life. I asked him did he really mean to say he had found peace in Islam? He said he had not at first, but now that he has joined a fraternity of dervishes, whose Sheikh is a truly pious, holy man, he has found perfect peace. I read to him several passages of the Bible, but he declined to read it for himself, or any other book I offered to lend him, saying, 'Why should I unsettle my mind again, now I have burned my bridges?' When I asked him to let me pray with him he refused, and said he would pray *for* me, but not with me. He was disappointed at my apparent unlikelihood of becoming a Moslem, but asked me to come to a religious meeting of the dervishes in the evening. I asked him if we should be allowed in? He said he had obtained special permission for us, as this was not like a mosque. I hesitated a moment, but he said we should be quite welcome; so I agreed to meet him at a café outside the city gate at one o'clock Turkish time (eight p.m.) When we arrived he met us in his dervish costume, a long white burnous, with a tall white fez cap, bound round with a white turban. He had with him a young Turkish officer, who spoke French, and who looked on with us and explained the proceedings. On arriving at the place, a house some distance outside the town, we left our shoes at the door, and were shown into a room with divans round the walls opening out of the courtyard where the exercises are carried on. In this room was seated the Sheikh, a man of about forty-five, with a long black beard, and a kind, mild look, that was very taking. He was small and extremely thin, dressed in a long white 'jebba' and the white burnous, and a very big white turban of the Egyptian form, with a broad black band part of the way round it. Several dervishes stood about in the room, and as fresh ones came in, they came and made a low obeisance to the Sheikh, and kissed his hand, and then placed it on their forehead, repeating it three times. He motioned to us to sit down, and to some of the others too. All these dervishes are Turks, but their religious exercises are carried on in Arabic, though very few understand that language. They are all very nice, well-bred fellows. Among them I recognised two or three young men from the custom-house, who came forward and spoke to us, seeming very glad to see us there, one offering us snuff, and another bringing us coffee. They brought one of the dervishes, a naval officer, who spoke a little English, to interpret for us to the Sheikh, and make our salutations, but his English was so weak that we tried Arabic, though with some difficulty. When about twenty-five or thirty dervishes had assembled, they went out into the courtyard to prayers, led by the Sheikh, all dressed in the white jebba, turban, and burnous (most, however, discarding the latter in the course of the proceedings), except one or two soldiers and a young negro. On the opposite roof of the courtyard we could see a party of veiled women watching it too. They first went through the regular prayers, repeating the Koran, and making the various prostrations simultaneously. Then they all sat round in a circle on the ground, with two of their number, little boys of twelve or fourteen in the middle, and the Sheikh in the corner. Then they began to repeat ' La Ilaha illa Allah ' (There is no God but God), at first slowly ; and then beginning to sway their bodies from side to side, they spoke quicker and louder every minute, until it became a hoarse roar of inarticulate sounds, their bodies thrown frantically from side to side and backwards and forwards, till one would think their backs would be dislocated. Sometimes they sat, sometimes knelt, and at other times stood, and so kept it up for some time. All this time one was chanting a kind of song, and I recognised the singer as A. E. of the custom-house. Then suddenly all was still, and the Sheikh commenced, in a low, musical voice, to sing some long extracts from the Koran. Then the collective repetition began again, this time only the word ' Allahu, Allahu,' until it became a hoarse roar, with the same frantic jerking of the body and head. Then the Sheikh came into the middle, and joined hands with the two little boys, and one after another joining the inner circle, they commenced to go round with a dancing step, they and the outer circle still keeping up the roar of ' Allahu, Allahu.' This went on for about an hour, A. E. still keeping up his song, sometimes accompanied, sometimes relieved by another. Then it all stopped, and the Sheikh led them again with the ordinary prayers and prostrations, then followed special prayers for all the saints of Islam, for the Sultan, and the Sheikh el Islam, ending up with the usual formula, ' There is no God but God,' etc. The performance was over about midnight, after two hours or more of the most frantic exertions. Then all came in again to the sitting-room, where the Sheikh took his seat, and gave us seats, while the others stood around. Two of our custom-house friends, who speak Arabic, then came and took it in turns to interpret for me into Turkish to the Sheikh, and we engaged in an exhaustive discussion of the truth of Islam, and I took the opportunity of telling the Sheikh the glad news of salvation. There was no excitement or heat of argument, but the quietest, most friendly discussion. At one point I took the opportunity to say, 'I have myself brought a message from God to you; He offers eternal life to whoever will accept it in His Son.' Turning to the whole company I said, 'If any man of you will come to God as dead in trespasses and sins, and condemned in His sight, will plead the death of Christ, His Son, in your stead, He will give you eternal life, the resurrection life of Christ.' The young man who interpreted for me faithfully translated what I said into Turkish, and they looked at one another, and then all at the Sheikh, who asked me what did I mean by 'plead his death'? I said, 'He died for my death, and He lives for my life.' My interpreter smilingly asked me would I die for them? I said to him, earnestly, 'I would, indeed, but I am but a sinful man, who cannot make satisfaction even for himself; but Christ, the only sinless One, died for the sins of the whole world; He could because He was the Son of God.' 'No,' said the Sheikh, 'he was born of Mary, by inspiration of the Angel Gabriel.' Here followed a discussion on the passage in the Koran, which they twisted to bear this meaning; as a matter of fact, the words are, 'We breathed into her of our spirit.' They asked me 'Was not the Koran the first revelation of God as the Merciful, the Compassionate, the only God?' I said, 'By no means;' the Gospel says, 'God so loved the world,' etc.; and then they all laughed at my interpreter's look of perplexity, at translating such a daring proposition to the Sheikh. They asked other questions, which gave me the opportunity of explaining fully what Christianity is. So it went on till nearly three o'clock; then I begged their pardon for having kept them so late, but I was so glad to get a chance of thus declaring the truth that I could not leave it imperfect. They said they were delighted; we must come again; they would be glad to see us every night! The Sheikh told me to come again and speak with him about these matters, and so we left, most of them accompanying us home. I told A. E. I would learn Turkish on purpose to facilitate my intercourse with them, and he said the Sheikh would like to see me alone if I could understand Turkish, as he speaks little or no Arabic, and he did not like to produce some arguments in the presence of the younger dervishes who might misunderstand him. The whole conversation had been in Arabic, the Lord opening my mouth wonderfully, quite to my own astonishment, but to His praise and glory."

We thank God for this opportunity; while at the same time it seems likely that the hope of converting our young friends to Islam is one reason for the great friendliness and forbearance shewn to them. The following extract from a recent letter shows touchingly how some of their Moslem friends desire to bring them to what they believe to be truth:—

"We have two young fellows who come here very often to discuss with me. We call them the Scribe and the Pharisee. We call them so because the former, whose name is M., is a great controversialist, and is always discussing the Law and the Prophets, and going into the philosophy of their religion, while the latter, S., is great at prayers, and all kinds of religious observances. Sometimes he stops M., and asks him what is the good of discussing all that, seeing we are blind because we *won't* see. Then he turns to me and says, 'Oh! Michell, what a fearful thing it will be for you when you will be in the fire, and you will remember your friend S., and wish you had listened to his words and believed in the Prophet,' etc. Then he urges me when it comes to my last moment just to say, 'There is no God but God, Mohammed is the Prophet of God,' etc., and if it is with my last breath the Prophet will accept it. He then tells me if I will not accept it myself, at least to tell the Tabib Effendi (Mr. Harding) what he says, so as to give him a chance. It is indeed quite a lesson to myself to see how earnestly and faithfully they preach their own religion, though unhappily it is such a false one."

In closing this short sketch of what has been done to take the Gospel to North Africa, let us again remember that the work is only commencing. A few lights have been placed here and there amid the thick darkness. Can the light penetrate? Will the darkness be dispelled? We look at the little band of light-bearers, and at the extent of the work to be done, and we say, Impossible! We look at the powers of evil arrayed against the truth: at the strength of human prejudices and long-cherished beliefs, earthly rulers hostile and ready to crush the unwelcome and intrusive novelty; we remember the unseen rulers of the darkness of this world putting forth all their power to hinder the entrance of the light, and again it seems impossible. But there comes to us the calm and reassuring voice of Him unto whom is given all power in heaven and on earth, and He says, "With men this is impossible, but with God all things are possible." If God be for us, who can be against us? Before Him the powers of darkness must fall; His own voice has called the weary and the heavy-laden to come to Him, and those that come He will in nowise cast out. "For He hath looked down from the height of His sanctuary; from heaven did the Lord behold the earth; to hear the groaning of the prisoner, to loose those that are appointed to death." His hand has wonderfully opened doors before His servants so far, and we believe that it is His gracious purpose to call many from those dark lands to join the great multitude who have washed their robes and made them white in the blood of the Lamb. "Pray ye therefore the Lord of the harvest that He would send forth labourers into His harvest."

www.ingramcontent.com/pod-product-compliance
Lightning Source LLC
Chambersburg PA
CBHW021919180426
43199CB00032B/928